The Moment of Exposure

Leon Levinstein

BOB SHAMIS
with an essay by Max Kozloff

The Moment of Exposure
Leon Levinstein

National Gallery of Canada
Ottawa, 1995

Published in conjunction with the exhibition **Leon Levinstein** organized by the National Gallery of Canada.

National Gallery of Canada, Ottawa
9 February–18 June 1995

Museum of Modern Art, New York
20 July–17 October 1995

Nickle Arts Museum, Calgary
3 November 1995–January 1996

Catalogue produced by the Publications Division of the National Gallery of Canada

Chief of Publications: Serge Thériault
Editors: Usher Caplan and Jacques Pichette
Picture Editor: Colleen Evans
Production Manager: Jean-Guy Bergeron
Designed by Angela Grauerholz, Montreal, with the assistance of Réjean Myette
Typeset in Formata by HB TechnoLith, Ottawa
Film by HB TechnoLith, Ottawa
Printed by HB TechnoLith, Ottawa, on Potlatch Quintessence Remarque paper

Available from your local bookseller or from
The Bookstore
National Gallery of Canada
380 Sussex Drive
Box 427, Station A
Ottawa, Canada
K1N 9N4

PRINTED IN CANADA

Photograph Credits

All copy photography National Gallery of Canada, with the exception of the following:

flap © Harvey Shaman, Kew Gardens, N.Y.
p. 13 (fig. 5) Herbert F. Johnson Museum of Art, Cornell University, Ithaca, N.Y.
p. 22 (fig. 11) Albright-Knox Art Gallery, Buffalo, N.Y.
p. 23 Syracuse University Art Collection, Syracuse, N.Y.
p. 53 David Lubarsky, New York, for the National Gallery of Canada
p. 69 Art Institute of Chicago
p. 76 Metropolitan Museum of Art, New York

Canadian Cataloguing in Publication Data

Shamis, Bob.
Leon Levinstein: The Moment of Exposure.
ISBN 0-88884-640-1

Issued also in French under the title: Leon Levinstein.
Le moment révélateur.
Exhibition catalogue.
1. Levinstein, Leon–Exhibitions.
2. Photography, Artistic–Exhibitions.
I. Kozloff, Max. II. National Gallery of Canada. III. Title.

TR647 L48 1995   770'.092   CIP 95-986000-2

CONTENTS

FOREWORD

In keeping with our tradition of making the National Gallery of Canada's collections accessible to the public and at the same time stimulating public awareness of the work of artists who, for one reason or another, are not as well known as they might be, we are proud to present this publication and its accompanying exhibition of the photographs of Leon Levinstein. It is the National Gallery's fourth retrospective exhibition of international photographers – beginning with Charles Nègre (1820–1880), Eugène Atget (1857–1927), and Lisette Model (1901–1983) – whose reputations we have helped to confirm if not establish.

Since 1967, we have been building a collection of photographs representative of the significant contributions photographers have made to the history of photography as an art form from 1839 to our own time. In 1990 we were able to add the work of Leon Levinstein. To the four examples we purchased in that year we were fortunate to add another twelve prints in 1992. This has been followed by a generous gift of 53 photographs from the artist's nephew and executor of the estate, Stuart E. Karu, made to the National Gallery through the kind auspices of the American Friends of Canada Committee. We are immensely grateful for this gift, for it is through the invaluable support of such civic-minded citizens that we are best able to build the Gallery's collections.

We are also indebted to Stuart Karu for his kindness in making Leon Levinstein's archives available to the National Gallery during the course of our preparation for this exhibition and for his willingness to lend so many works to it.

Without the generous support of other collectors, the exhibition would not have been possible. For having lent works we are beholden to Martin Bondell and Juliette Galant; John Erdman and Gary Schneider; Dr. Barry Ramer; the Art Institute of Chicago; the Brick Store Museum, Kennebunk, Maine; the Dreyfus Corporation, New York; Hallmark Cards, Incorporated, Kansas City; the Sander Gallery, New York; and the Metropolitan Museum of Art, New York. These individuals and institutions have made it possible for us to celebrate Leon Levinstein's unique and profound expression of the human condition.

Our guest curator, Bob Shamis, has brought his valuable research skills and sensitive understanding to bear on this project, abundantly apparent in his essay "Leon Levinstein: His Life and Photographs." We also wish to thank Max Kozloff for sharing with us through his essay, "Leon Levinstein and the School of New York," his moving and insightful perception of a passionate artist.

Dr. Shirley L. Thomson
Director
National Gallery of Canada

PREFACE

In the spring of 1989 Howard Greenberg, whose photography gallery had been chosen to represent the estate of Leon Levinstein, engaged me to organize the Levinstein archives. The photographs, thousands of them, were in total disarray, falling out of old, crumbling Kodak and Agfa photo paper boxes whose contents rarely bore any relation to their labels. To make matters worse, the space that had been rented for this undertaking was hopelessly cramped. When I expressed my frustration to Howard, he encouraged me to continue, assuring me that I would soon find it worthwhile and that I would be amazed by the strength of the work. I have been echoing Howard's ardent appreciation of Leon Levinstein's photographs ever since. By the time I entered graduate school that fall, I had resolved to find a way to organize a Levinstein retrospective. Two years later, based on a proposal to research Levinstein's life and the influences on his work, I was awarded the Lisette Model/Joseph G. Blum Fellowship in Photography by the Canadian Centre for the Visual Arts at the National Gallery of Canada. It was soon after my tenure there that I raised the possibility of an exhibition and publication.

That my vision of a Levinstein retrospective was finally brought to realization is due in large measure to the efforts of numerous individuals who contributed their time and energies to this project. I want to begin by thanking Leon Levinstein's nephew Stuart Karu, whom Leon entrusted with his photographic legacy. Without hesitation, Mr. Karu generously and unrestrictedly made the contents of the Levinstein archives available to me for my research and for the exhibition. Other family members who assisted greatly by shedding light on the personal history of this solitary man included his sister, Bernice Karu; his brother, the late Morton Levinstein, and his wife Sonny; his niece Joan Levinstein; and his cousins Beatrice Conn, Jason Rappeport, Stanley Rappeport, and Theodore Schuchat. Mr. Schuchat not only provided significant information about Leon's first years in New York but also furnished clues relating to certain periods in Leon's life for which I had no other source. Additional background information on the Levinstein family was provided by Perce Ross of Buckhannon, West Virginia; Noel Tenney of the Upshur County Historical Society, Buckhannon; and Virginia R. North, Archivist, Jewish Historical Society of Maryland, Baltimore.

Friends and colleagues of Levinstein who generously gave of their time in interviews and telephone conversations included Jerry Carr, Adam Cohen, Jem Cohen, Miriam Grossman Cohen, Jerry Danzig, John Ebstel, Max Falk, Douglas Fraser, Bruce Gilden, Allen Hochman, Eleanor and the late Ray Jacobs, Sy Kattelson, Gary Lapow, Marcelle Lapow, Carl Naylor, Victor Obsatz, Patrick Pagnano, Arthur Porta, Leon Schnall, Paul Seligman, Larry Siegel, Simon Stanislow, and David Vestal. I would especially like to express my appreciation to Adam and Jem Cohen for having had the foresight to record a wide-ranging interview with Leon in the summer of 1988, and for making this invaluable resource available to me. Other individuals who shared their memories and impressions of Leon included Helen Gee, John Gossage, Howard Greenberg, Maria Morris Hambourg, Susan Kismaric, Helen Levitt, Grace Mayer, Wayne Miller, and Sandra Phillips. I also want to thank Bob Cato for his description of the classes and teaching methods of Alexey Brodovitch, and Anne Tucker, Curator of Photography, Museum of Fine Arts, Houston, for generously sharing her knowledge of Sid Grossman and the Photo League.

The following individuals, institutions, and galleries provided professional support and assistance: William Johnson; Vivien Knussi; J. Russell Harris, Assistant to the Curator, and Sylvia Wolf and Colin Westerbeck, Associate Curators, Art Institute of Chicago; Marcia

Tiedes, Cataloguer, Center for Creative Photography, Tucson; Jeffrey Rosenheim, Curatorial Assistant, Metropolitan Museum of Art, New York; Helen Ennis, former Curator of Photography, Australian National Gallery, Canberra; Thom Sempere, Curatorial Assistant, San Francisco Museum of Modern Art; the Photography Study Center, Museum of Modern Art, New York; Martha R. Severens, former Curator of Collections, Portland Museum of Art, Portland, Maine; Kathryn A. Hussey, Registrar, Brick Store Museum, Kennebunk, Maine; G. Thomas Tanselle, Vice-President, John Simon Guggenheim Memorial Foundation, New York; Rachel Stuhlman, Librarian, Becky Simmons, Associate Librarian, and Tracey Lemon, Technical Services Librarian, International Museum of Photography and Film, George Eastman House, Rochester, New York; Keith F. Davis, Fine Arts Program Director, Hallmark Cards, Incorporated, Kansas City; Patti Sabatini, Dreyfus Corporation; Gerd Sander, Eleanor Barefoot, and Alejandro Saralegui, Sander Gallery, New York; and the entire staff of the Howard Greenberg Gallery, but especially Alix Mellis, whose assistance was indispensable to the organization of the exhibition.

At the National Gallery of Canada there were innumerable people who contributed their time and talents to this exhibition and catalogue. I was extremely fortunate to have had Joanne Larocque-Poirier as project manager. Many thanks as well to Daniel Lohnes of Design Services; Anne Newlands of the Education Division, John McElhone, Conservator of Photographs; and Kate Laing from Registration. For their skillful work on the catalogue, I am grateful to the staff of the Publications Division, in particular Usher Caplan and Jacques Pichette, editors of the English and French editions respectively; Colleen Evans, Picture Editor; Jean-Guy Bergeron, Production Manager; and Serge Thériault, Chief of Publications. My thanks also to Angela Grauerholz for her insightful design work on this catalogue.

As guest curator, I was treated with extreme cordiality by the staff of the Photographs Collection. I want to thank Barbara Boutin and Hazel Mackenzie for all their assistance. Lori Pauli's contribution went far beyond that of being a superb curatorial assistant – handling inquiries and requests, researching details, and generally keeping things under control in ways too numerous to mention. James Borcoman's unwavering support for this project has meant a great deal, and his comments and suggestions have certainly enhanced the quality of this exhibition. Ann Thomas very generously shared her knowledge of Lisette Model and American photography in the years after World War II. I value our conversations about Model and Levinstein as much for their far-ranging digressions as for what was relevant to my research. Even more valued is the friendship and hospitality of Ann and her husband, Brydon Smith, which helped me survive the coldest winter I ever want to experience.

Finally, I want to thank my wife, Dagmar, who through no choice of her own has lived with the joys and trials of this project for as long as I have.

Bob Shamis

Leon Levinstein

His Life and Photographs

BOB SHAMIS

Many people knew Leon Levinstein. Many of these same people admitted that they knew hardly anything about him. More than two years after his death, people who had once been close friends did not know that he had died. Most friends and colleagues in New York knew virtually nothing about the first half of his life in West Virginia and Baltimore. His family in Baltimore knew little more about the forty years he spent in New York. And neither family nor friends seemed to know anything about the personal details of his life. Large gaps in his personal history form a conspicuous void. Most likely there are certain facts – certain events or relationships – which, if revealed, would help us better understand the man and his art. However, beyond his photographs, the clues he left behind are minimal. There is also the possibility that this void is a sign – the sign of an extraordinary solitude.

The one thing about Leon Levinstein of which we can be certain is that for nearly forty years he made photographs; when he was not sleeping, or eating, or working as a graphic designer, he was walking the streets of New York, or whatever city he was in, and photographing. Of those who saw his photographs, there were few who were not greatly impressed. Yet, like the rest of his life, the esteem he earned as a photographer has, until very recently, remained a well-kept secret.

In the first decade of his career, spanning the 1950s, Levinstein was published numerous times in the major photography magazines, he was included in seven exhibitions at the Museum of Modern Art in New York, he had work exhibited in Europe and Japan, and he had a one-person show at the Limelight Gallery, which at the time was the one important photography gallery in New York. Yet by the time of his death in 1988, although he had continued to photograph until the mid-1980s, he was relatively unknown, even

Fig. 1
Paul Strand
Photograph – New York 1916
Photogravure printed 1917
22.2 × 16.8 cm
National Gallery of Canada

Fig. 2
Lewis Hine
Young Spinner in Carolina Mill:
Child Labor 1908
Gelatin silver print
12.6 × 17.6 cm
National Gallery of Canada

within the photographic community. Levinstein was not a man who either sought or was content with obscurity. He very much wanted recognition and respect as an artist, and he strongly believed that he deserved it. Naively, perhaps, he thought that the photographs should speak for themselves.

And undeniably his photographs speak with a powerful voice. However, an artist's renown seldom rests solely on the quality of his work. Levinstein's reluctance to promote himself and his uneasy relationships with galleries and photography dealers have sometimes been attributed to an uncompromising integrity and distrust of the "art world." He also had a reputation of being quarrelsome and hard to deal with. Whatever the reasons, the fact is that numerous times in his life he made things very difficult for people who were trying to further his career.

In an odd way, his photographs created their own difficulties for his career and recognition. For although virtually all of his photographs are images of people, they refuse to fit neatly into categories. Levinstein did candid street portraiture, or "street photography," a form of documentary photography that has been practiced for nearly a century [fig. 1] and which flourished in urban America in the 1950s and '60s. However, it is exceedingly difficult to consider many of Levinstein's images as documents. On the other hand, these strong graphic and formal statements refuse to be viewed as purely interesting abstractions. Within the forms we find stories and people's lives. Levinstein's blend of document and form and emotion may have been unique, but in many ways it epitomized some of the strongest currents running through American photography after World War II.

Fig. 3
Walker Evans
Mrs. Frank Tengle, Wife of a
Cotton Sharecropper, Hale
County, Alabama 1936
Gelatin silver print
19.8 × 7.3 cm
National Gallery of Canada

Fig. 4
Aaron Siskind
Untitled, from *Harlem*
Document 1937
Gelatin silver print
35.5 × 27.7 cm
National Gallery of Canada

Fig. 5
Philip Evergood
Pink Dismissal Slip 1937
Oil on masonite panel
71.1 × 55.9 cm
Herbert F. Johnson Museum
of Art, Cornell University,
Ithaca, N.Y., gift of
Harry N. Abrams

Although "documentary photography" is much too limiting as a description of Levinstein's images, it is still a term extremely relevant to his work. For regardless of their appearance, it is out of the spirit and tradition of documentary photography in America that Levinstein's photographs derive. His pictures are clearly documentary in the sense that they are unstaged, uncontrived images of people in the world. Without question, they present the "stark record" that Walker Evans felt was the defining quality of the documentary style.[1] If, due to their intense and unabashed subjectivity, at times radical framing, or dramatic rendering of form, we hesitate to characterize his photographs as documentary, our reluctance is as much a commentary on the transformation of that tradition as it is about Levinstein's work.

In the years immediately following World War II, the practice of documentary photography in America was changing significantly. Until the war, it had been most closely associated with the depiction of social problems and promoting reform, as in the photographs of Jacob Riis and Lewis Hine [fig. 2] and the work done for the Farm Security Administration in the 1930s as well as other work that arose out of the FSA project [fig. 3]. The documentary work of the Photo League in New York City [fig. 4] extended the socially-concerned reform tradition of Riis and Hine. By the mid-1940s, however, these grounds for photographing were losing their appeal and no longer served to inspire very many photographers, especially those who were just then becoming involved with photography. The members of this newer generation sought to depict in their work neither "objective reality" nor the justification for a social or political program, regardless of how well-meaning. Instead, they wanted to express a personal response to the world in which they lived.

There were many factors that contributed to this change in attitude, and these were primarily, but

1.   William Stott, *Documentary Expression and Thirties America* (New York: Oxford University Press, 1973), p. 269.

2.   Social Realism was probably the dominant movement in painting in the United States in the 1930s. Although Social Realist painting was always figurative and often narrative, it encompassed a large variety of formal and pictorial approaches. More thematically than stylistically unified, the painters in this group insisted on an art that communicated ideas and expressed social values. They attempted to call attention to social injustice and capitalist exploitation by portraying the lives of the poor and working class people, more specifically "the misery of unemployment, the fortitude of workers, the corruption of the ruling class and the humiliation caused by poverty." Phillip Evergood, William Gropper, Jacob Lawrence, and Ben Shahn are a few of the better known

not entirely, related to World War II and its aftermath. First, this change mirrored the general inward turning of artists, visual and otherwise, in response to the devastation of the war. It was also a reflection of a growing cynicism and disillusionment about involvement with mass political movements and the possibility of effecting meaningful political change. Many photographers and artists sympathetic to socialism and the Communist government in Russia were shocked and dismayed by Stalin's pact with Hitler in 1939 and later by revelations about Stalin's oppression of his own people. Their withdrawal from the political sphere was only compounded by the anti-Communist hysteria and more general conservative course that the country took in the late '40s and early '50s. The rapid decline of the Social Realist style of painting [fig. 5] in the United States after World War II was one sign of this retreat.[2] Also, more than ever before, the veracity of the photo-document was open to skepticism as a result of the use of photographs as a propaganda tool by both sides during the war. As early as 1940 in his column in *PM's Weekly*, the Sunday magazine of the New York newspaper *PM*, the photographer and editor Ralph Steiner was analyzing – today we would say deconstructing – Nazi propaganda photographs. He was also writing articles with titles such as "What Is Truth in Photography?"[3] Finally, there was the growing influence of certain European photographers such as André Kertész, Brassaï, Henri Cartier-Bresson [fig. 6], and Lisette Model. Unlike most American photographers of that era, they were comfortable with the notion that their photography, both in content and in style, was an expression of their personal view of the world, and they had no qualms about acknowledging aesthetic concerns in their work.[4] Evident in the imagery of these photographers, and increasingly evident in the work of some American photographers, was a certain tension, a "contest of meaning" between subject matter, the

Social Realists. Many of the ideals and political sympathies of the Social Realist painters were shared by members of the Photo League (discussed later in this essay), especially prior to World War II. See David Shapiro, "Social Realism Reconsidered," in *Social Realism: Art as a Weapon*, ed. David Shapiro (New York: Fredrick Ungar, 1973), p. 13.

3.	Carol Payne, "Challenging 'Truth': Ralph Steiner's Analysis of Nazi Propaganda at *PM's Weekly*," an unpublished address to the Frick Symposium, Institute of Fine Arts, New York University, 13 April 1992.

4.	I am referring here to the noncommercial work of these photographers.

thing photographed, and the way in which it was photographed. As Peter Collins has written in noting this change of attitude: "The details of the real world maintained their predominance as the carriers of symbol, but their relationships became more relative, ambiguous, and insular. The documentary photograph became recognized not as a surrogate of the world, but as an analog to it, a personal prescription."[5] It was at this very critical and fertile juncture in documentary photography that Leon Levinstein, for reasons he never revealed, decided to study photography and, within a few years, to devote his life to it.

Fig. 6
Henri Cartier-Bresson
Roman Amphitheatre,
Valencia, Spain 1933
Gelatin silver print
15.8 × 23.8 cm
National Gallery of Canada

Leon Levinstein was born on 20 September 1910 in Buckhannon, West Virginia, a small college town with a population of about five thousand.[6] His father, Simon, was a Lithuanian Jew who first visited Buckhannon in the summer of 1890 at the age of fifteen. Simon would take the train west from Baltimore to West Virginia and then walk from town to town selling merchandise from a pack on his back. After five years as an itinerant peddler, he opened a "dry goods" store in Hyattsville, Maryland. He remained there for three years and evidently prospered. Then, in the summer of 1898, he moved to Buckhannon and opened the Enterprise Clothing Store, which offered "Great bargains in Clothing, Boots, Shoes, Hats, Gents furnishing goods. Everything up to date."[7] His business grew steadily, and in 1912 he expanded, opening Levinstein's Department Store, which for the next twenty-five years was the largest business in the town.

On one of his regular trips to Baltimore to visit relatives and order goods for his store, he was introduced to Ida Rappeport, one of eight children of Orthodox Jewish immigrants and also from Lithuania. They were married in Baltimore in 1905, and after the wedding they returned to Buckhannon to live. In 1906 they had their first child, a son, Morton. Leon was born in 1910, followed by another son, Eli, in 1911. Their fourth child was a girl, Bernice, born in 1916.

Leon rarely spoke of his family or of his childhood, but when he did, he recalled his early years in Buckhannon with fondness.[8] The Levinsteins were Orthodox Jews, and the Levinstein boys celebrated their bar mitzvahs. Beyond that, religion does not seem to have played an important role in their family life. Although they were the only Jewish family in a small southern town, Levinstein never mentioned experiencing any overt prejudice or sense of being ostracized while growing up in Buckhannon, and his brother Morton remembered that they were accepted and treated well there. Their father, Simon, was not only a

5.   Peter Collins, wall text for *New Standpoints*, an exhibition at the Museum of Modern Art, New York, February 1978.

6.   County Clerk's Office, Upshur County, W. Va., Birth Book 4, p. 96. Despite the evidence of these records, several relatives have stated that they believe he was born in 1908. Sometime in the 1950s Levinstein started giving 1913 as the year of his birth. David Vestal suggests that he may have decided to take several years off his age when he first applied for a Guggenheim Fellowship, for 1955. Ironically, it was to be another twenty years before he would be awarded a Guggenheim.

7.   French Morgan, *Yesterdays of Buckhannon and Upshur* (Buckhannon, W. Va.: The Buckhannon Delta, 1963), p. 30.

8.   Interview with Douglas Fraser and Allen Hochman, 15 January 1992. Fraser worked as a photographer and Hochman as studio manager at Brown & Gravenson, the catalogue merchandising firm where Levinstein worked as art director from 1968 to 1973.

successful businessman, but was also well liked and respected in Buckhannon. He seems to have assimilated easily into the life of the town, becoming a member of some local fraternal organizations, including the Masons. Being separated from family and the close-knit Jewish community of Baltimore may not have bothered Simon or the Levinstein children, but it took its toll on Ida Levinstein. There was little in Buckhannon that appealed to her, and she visited Baltimore frequently. Finally, in 1923, Ida and the children moved to Baltimore, ostensibly to take advantage of the better educational opportunities available there for her children. By then, probably because of his drawing, Leon was already known in Buckhannon as "the artistic one" in the Levinstein family.[9]

The Levinsteins moved into a large house on Cedric Road in Walbrook, a quiet, attractive, ethnically diverse, middle-class community in northwest Baltimore.[10] For the next twenty years, Simon Levinstein would travel between Buckhannon and Baltimore, devoting most of his time to his business and seeing his wife and family only once or twice each month. Leon began attending high school in September 1923 at Baltimore City College, which was not a college in the usual sense, but a public college-preparatory school. He took all the academic courses expected of a student planning to go on to college, but his grades were no better than average. Only in his art courses did he excel.

Although shy and asocial, Levinstein was not a total recluse during his high school years. He had a number of friends, and enjoyed sports, especially basketball. Most of the time, however, he would be off on his own. One of his cousins, Beatrice Conn, recalls that he enjoyed hiking alone in the parks and woods of suburban Baltimore.[11] After school he usually would go up to his room on the third floor, close the door, and draw for hours on end, without ever showing his drawings to anyone. Once when his brother Morton came into his room and asked to see what he was doing, Leon turned towards him and angrily hurled his drawing board, barely missing him and making a large hole in the bedroom wall.[12]

The Levinsteins did not foster an interest in cultural enrichment in their home, and Leon did not receive any encouragement for his artistic pursuits. To his mostly conservative, middle-class Jewish relatives, he was known variously as "the arty one," "the oddball," or "the black sheep" of the family, depending on whom you asked. Beatrice Conn recalled a particular episode that presages Levinstein's wanderlust and illustrates the gulf between Leon and his family: right after graduating from high school, he enlisted in the Merchant Marine, and when his parents found out, they objected vehemently and made a trip to New York to extricate him from his commitment.[13]

During his senior year in high school, he began attending evening classes at the Maryland Institute of Art in Baltimore. In the fall of 1927, after graduating from high school, he enrolled as a part-time student at the Institute, taking courses in drawing, calligraphy, and design. He withdrew after one year. Nobody seems able to recall where he was or what he was doing during the subsequent five years. His sister has vague memories of his having

9.   Interview with Perce Ross, 20 January 1992. Ross, a resident of Buckhannon, knew the Levinstein family. In his youth he had worked briefly at Levinstein's Department Store.

10.   Interview with Virginia R. North, Archivist, Jewish Historical Society of Maryland, Baltimore, 11 August 1994.

11.   Interview with Beatrice Conn, 18 November 1991.

12.   Interview with Morton Levinstein, 18 November 1991.

13.   Conn interview.

gone to Pittsburgh to study art. In his application for a 1955 Guggenheim Fellowship he mentions taking courses at the Art Institute of Pittsburgh; no school records for the period could be found to confirm this, but in light of his subsequent career as a graphic artist it is reasonable to assume that he did study there, as it was primarily a commercial art school.

By the fall of 1933 Levinstein was once again enrolled in an evening drawing class at the Maryland Institute of Art, and a few months later he began what was probably his first job in advertising, with the Hecht Furniture Company in downtown Baltimore. From 1934 to 1937 he worked there as an assistant art director, doing layouts for newspaper advertisements. He then set out on his own as a freelance graphic artist and designer. The year 1937 was certainly not an ideal time to be starting a small business in America, and it is hardly surprising that Levinstein also supported himself working as a salesman for a graphics and photo-engraving company in Baltimore called Advertising Art & Engraving Services. He held this job until 1942, when he enlisted in the army. During the war he was stationed for most of the time in Panama, serving as a propeller repair mechanic with the Air Corps. His tour of duty was uneventful, and he was discharged with the rank of sergeant in October 1945.

Levinstein returned to Baltimore, but he was to remain there for only a few months. Bernard Kramer, a friend who had been in the advertising business in Baltimore for many years, was moving to New York to start his own agency, and he recruited Levinstein to work for him. Also joining them was Levinstein's younger cousin Theodore Schuchat. Kramer was to be the accounts executive, Levinstein the art director, and Schuchat the copywriter.

After the war there was a severe housing shortage in New York, and so the two cousins got rooms at a once-bustling downtown hotel, the Broadway Central, then located on Broadway a few blocks north of Houston Street. Schuchat recalls that at the time they were living there it was a "raffish establishment, definitely going downhill." After a few months they were able to move into a small, two-bedroom "bathtub-in-the-kitchen" tenement apartment on Thompson Street in the predominantly Italian neighborhood in the heart of Greenwich Village. The rent was $18 a month.[14]

The Colby Advertising Agency, named after the cafeteria where the three would meet until they were able to find office space, was eventually located in a small office building at the corner of 52nd Street and Fifth Avenue in midtown Manhattan. Its principal client was Edward Morris, "The Square Deal Jeweler," who owned a large and apparently very successful chain of discount jewelry stores throughout Pennsylvania, Maryland, and Delaware. Morris was a firm believer in advertising, and his business kept Colby Advertising afloat. Levinstein was in charge of the art work – he did all of the design and layouts, hiring freelance artists to draw the jewelry. Layouts were to be his forte throughout his career in advertising [fig. 7].

Having a job in New York provided Levinstein with the opportunity to get away from his family and to further his art studies. In an interview given shortly before his death in 1988, Levinstein in fact claimed that he had come to New York in order to study painting.[15] Between 1947 and 1951 he studied art as a part-time evening student at the New School for Social Research. During these years he took several studio courses, including painting

14.   Interview with Theodore Schuchat, 19 November 1991.

15.   Leon Levinstein, in a tape-recorded interview by Adam and Jem Cohen, 1988, hereinafter referred to as Levinstein interview.

Fig. 7
Leon Levinstein
Catalogue layout for Bulova
watches, n.d.

with Stuart Davis and printmaking with Louis Schanker, and attended lectures in contemporary art and aesthetics. However, one of the first classes he enrolled in was a photography course taught by the innovative and extremely influential graphic designer and art director Alexey Brodovitch. Over the years, Brodovitch would count among his students Richard Avedon, Bruce Davidson, Hiro, Irving Penn, and numerous other highly-regarded professional photographers and graphic designers.

In the late 1940s Brodovitch taught a course titled "Art Applied to Graphic Journalism," comprised of two sections, design and photography. Although students could take both sections, the enrollment was separate for each class. Given Brodovitch's reputation as an art director and designer, it is not surprising that Levinstein chose to study with him. However, we can only speculate why, when he was just starting to build a career as a graphic artist, he chose to enroll in the photography section.

Before moving to New York in 1946, Levinstein had not demonstrated any special interest in photography. In 1941 or 1942, prior to entering the army, he had purchased a camera from a Jewish refugee from Germany. The man had several cameras to sell, and Levinstein chose a 2 1/4 inch square format Rolleiflex. According to an account he gave in 1956, he chose this particular camera simply because he liked the sound of the name.[16] The only surviving photographs that predate his arrival in New York are some portraits of his parents [fig. 8] probably made towards the end of 1945, shortly after his discharge from the army.

As a teacher, Brodovitch was provocative and confrontational. At the opening meeting of one of his courses in the early 1960s, he told his students: "We must communicate. We must expose ourselves . . . I hate imitations and clichés . . . My way of guiding people is by irritation. I will try to irritate you, to explore you . . . You should provoke me, and only then can I provoke you back."[17] One former student recalled: "Two thirds of the students felt rejected and became defensive and withdrawn. One third took up the

16.   "Leon Levinstein," *U.S. Camera 1956*, p. 255.

17.   Andy Grundberg, *Brodovitch* (New York: Harry N. Abrams, 1989), pp. 138, 140.

challenge."[18] Levinstein, apparently, was among the latter. As Schuchat recalls: "To the extent that Leon spoke to me in those days, he spoke about Brodovitch. 'Brodovitch is terrific . . . I'm learning so much from Brodovitch . . . He critiqued my pictures tonight.' . . . To the extent that he had a mentor at that time, it was Brodovitch."[19]

As the art director at *Harper's Bazaar*, Brodovitch was primarily involved with fashion photography. Yet at the same time he appreciated the immediacy and impact of candid, available-light photography, and over the years he championed the work of Bill Brandt, Brassaï, Cartier-Bresson, Robert Frank, and Lisette Model in the pages of one of the world's leading fashion magazines. Bob Cato, a photographer who assisted him in his classes, recalls: "Brodovitch encouraged involved street photography, not observation. He wanted you to 'go beyond the glass' and focus your life on that one moment on the street."[20] He told his students: "Develop a statement of your own. Shout, don't whisper."[21] Levinstein characterized his own work in strikingly similar terms: "One thing I always try to do, if possible, is never to speak mildly or softly. I don't think any photographer should . . . It should be loud and clear."[22] As Andy Grundberg has noted: "Intuition and feeling were precisely what Brodovitch treasured in photographs, and what he tried to teach photographers to treasure as well . . . their pictures could be personally expressive and documentary. What mattered to him was not the technique used to achieve the picture, or even its style, but its effect. It had to be bold, shocking, and close to the photographer's skin."[23]

Studying with Brodovitch certainly provided a strong impetus to Levinstein's development as a photographer, and if we look at the graphic and emotionally expressive photographs he produced over the next thirty-five years, the influence of the Brodovitch philosophy is evident. However, it would take a few more years, and the strong influence of

18.   Ibid., p. 138 (quoting the photographer Bob Adelman).
19.   Schuchat interview
20.   Interview with Bob Cato, February 1992.
21.   Claire Steinberg, "Alexey Brodovitch: 1900—1971," in *Photography Annual 1972*, p. 168.
22.   Levinstein interview.
23.   Grundberg, p. 120.

another critical and demanding teacher, Sid Grossman, before Levinstein's photographs were to have the dynamism and formal strength we now associate with his work.

At about the same time that Levinstein was studying with Brodovitch, he was introduced to the Photo League by a young man who worked under him in the art department at Colby Advertising. The Photo League was an organization based in New York made up primarily of socially-concerned documentary photographers. It had evolved out of the politically more radical New York Film and Foto League of the 1930s, and many of its members still championed a leftist political agenda. By the late 1940s, however, the primary concern of the Photo League and the chief interest of most of its members was photography, not politics.[24] Even in the late '30s and early '40s, the gallery of the Photo League was already exhibiting a very broad range of creative photography, including the work of Eugène Atget, Manuel Alvarez Bravo, László Moholy-Nagy, Lisette Model, and Edward Weston. After the war, Ansel Adams and Nancy and Beaumont Newhall, never considered stalwarts of the radical left, not only lectured at the League but also contributed articles to Photo Notes, the League's highly-regarded monthly publication.[25]

One of the most important components of the Photo League was its school, which in the late '40s was the only professional photography school in the United States not geared towards advertising work or other forms of commercial photography. At the time, photography was included in the curriculum of only three or four university art departments. In 1947 Levinstein enrolled in an introductory course taught by John Ebstel in which he learned the basics of developing and printing. In the fall of 1948 he took an advanced workshop with the school's director and one of its most influential teachers, Sid Grossman. Beginning in the early '40s, but especially after the war, Grossman, who had previously photographed in what can only be characterized as a straightforward documentary style [fig. 9], had begun to approach photography – both in his own work and in his teaching – as a means of personal expression. As early as 1943 Grossman had stated: "We of the Photo League urge our pupils . . . to think only of the convincing power of reality plus the power of your own personal statement" and "Photography can

---

24.   A great deal of the activity at the Photo League after World War II involved people like Levinstein who took classes at the school and attended lectures and exhibitions but were never members. They simply wanted to learn about photography and use the facilities, such as the darkroom. Given the middle-class and lower-middle-class urban Jewish background of many of them, they were likely to have been politically liberal and perhaps sympathetic to leftist causes. Most, however, were less politically committed than the members at the time, who themselves were generally less committed than the members prior to World War II.

25.   For a reprint of the entire series, see *Photo Notes, February 1938–Spring 1950 / Filmfront, December 1934–March 1935* (Rochester: Visual Studies Workshop, 1977).

Fig. 10
Leon Levinstein
Untitled 1951
Gelatin silver print
23.0 × 30.0 cm
Stuart E. Karu

be expressive of the strongest human feelings, including those of the photographer himself."[26]

In December 1947 the Photo League was included on Attorney General Tom Clark's list of "totalitarian, Fascist, Communist, or subversive" organizations. Despite an initial out-pouring of support by photographers and other artists and intellectuals, the League closed its doors in 1951. Grossman had been a member of the Communist Party, and according to his widow, Miriam Grossman Cohen, he was being singled out for special attention and harassment by the FBI. By the summer of 1949 he had left the Photo League. Ironically, during the last years of his association with the League, Grossman had come under increasing criticism from some of its more politically radical members for advocating a view of photography as a medium of artistic expression. Encouraged by his former students and desperately in need of income as a result of being blacklisted, he continued teaching a weekly workshop in his 24th Street loft.[27] Levinstein attended Grossman's classes regularly for the following three years, and his experience in the workshop and the ideas he was exposed to formed the core of his approach to photography for the rest of his life.

Sid Grossman is remembered as having been "an incredible teacher . . . remarkably underappreciated . . . brilliant" but at the same time "bitter . . . intimidating . . . a destructive teacher [who] would decimate students' work in critiques."[28] Like Brodovitch, Grossman was sharply confrontational, and he constantly tested his students' commitment to photography. One of his primary goals was to break down what he considered lazy, habitual modes of seeing and conventional ways of using the camera. But for Grossman, it was not just the final image and its effect that mattered. Photography was an act of transformation and revelation demanding emotional involvement: "If every picture is something that concerns you very directly and intimately and very passionately – if you are not ashamed of that – then the result will be a revelation to you."[29] His most damning and persistent criticism of photographs was that they did not derive from a direct emotional response to the subject. He told his class: "No one creates anything new and anything good without a certain amount of passion, and you do not create out of a formula."[30]

Grossman's classes have been likened by some of his former students to group therapy, involving "tremendous exposure of peoples' psyches."[31] In actual fact, a great deal of class time was devoted to the analysis of photographs and to wide-ranging intellectual discussion. Grossman himself was very clear as to what the classes were about: "We have to learn to talk about what we are doing. We have to learn to analyze, to evaluate our experience and take these experiences and put them together and draw some conclusions from an intelligent conversation, and to use these tools for making progress in our develop-ment as photographers."[32] Ann Treer, a student of Grossman's, recalled: "Usually, we would

26.   Quoted by Jacob Deschin, in "Flash! Camera Club Carries Out Program," *Popular Photography,* February 1943, pp. 54, 93.

27.   Interview with Miriam Grossman Cohen, 26 January 1991.

28.   Interview with Ray and Eleanor Jacobs, 13 November 1991.

29.   From a transcript by Ann Winters of wire recordings made in Grossman's class by Harry Lapow in the spring of 1950, hereinafter referred to as Winters transcript.

30.   Winters transcript.

31.   Eleanor Jacobs interview.

32.   Winters transcript.

go on past midnight, well past midnight, with Sid constantly urging and shocking us into articulating what we thought, and then he would proceed to cut away the fog."[33]

Throughout his life Levinstein shied away from making any comments on his own photographs. When asked about any particular photograph, he would at most respond with an anecdote about the circumstances in which he had taken it. He once wrote: "[I] hate wordy explanations and pseudo-intellectual comments on one's photography."[34] Yet the primary activities of Grossman's classes consisted of intellectualizing the experience of being a photographer and analyzing photographs and discussing them within an aesthetic and intellectual context; for three years Leon attended these classes religiously, and for another three years he would often stop by Grossman's loft late Friday evening and sit in on the end of a class.

Levinstein's experience as a student of drawing and painting undoubtedly helped shape his approach to photography. However, when he started taking classes with Grossman he was still as tentative in his photographic image-making as any typical beginner [fig. 10].[35] Levinstein had been drawing since he was an adolescent, and he painted and took art classes from the age of fourteen until he was into his fifties, attending Evsa Model's painting workshop from about 1954 until 1960. He was, by all accounts, never very accomplished as a painter,[36] and, according to several friends, once he had become seriously committed to photography, he painted only for fun and relaxation. Still, it is not surprising that many of his strongest photographs, although always springing from his spontaneous observations of people, seem to reflect some of the same formal and expressive issues that had concerned the Social Realists. Several of his photographs call to mind the paintings of the American artist Ben Shahn in their use of simplified or abstracted human forms to articulate a very subjective and emotionally expressive realism [figs. 11, 12].

An examination of Levinstein's photographs in relation to the work of some of the artists he studied with, such as Stuart Davis, Evsa Model, and Louis Schanker, does not reveal any strong affinities. There seems to be a much clearer connection with certain aspects of the work of artists he admired: the subjectivity and emotional intensity of Francis Bacon and Edvard Munch, and the rendering of the human figure by Reginald Marsh.[37] Levinstein and Marsh both found most of their subjects by walking the streets of New York City. Both were fascinated by the relaxed and open display of flesh and intimacy

33.   Les Barry, "The Legend of Sid Grossman," *Popular Photography*, November 1961, p. 93.

34.   Artist's notebook, unpaginated and undated, courtesy of Stuart Karu.

35.   Interviews with David Vestal, 21 March 1991, and Sy Kattelson, 8 February 1992.

36.   No paintings from his classes at the New School or from Evsa Model's workshop (where he used tempera paint on newsprint) have survived. Eleanor Jacobs remembers his paintings from Model's class as "large masses of primary color." An old friend, Leon Schnall (interview, 6 July 1991), described Levinstein's painting as resembling the work of Hans Hoffman. Another friend, Jerry Carr (interview, 6 April 1992), recalls that in the 1960s Levinstein would paint on the floor of his apartment on masonite or scraps of seamless studio background paper. He never signed his paintings. Although Carr remembers seeing ten to fifteen paintings on masonite leaning against the wall in Levinstein's apartment, only one (in Carr's possession) has been located.

37.   Levinstein interview.

at Coney Island, and went back there repeatedly during the course of their artistic careers.[38] The thing that impressed Levinstein most about Marsh was his ability to create such sensually expressive human forms [fig. 13]. Tied to reality and denied the painter's license to exaggerate, the photographer, in Levinstein's view, was faced with a much more difficult challenge, though one that he himself often met with considerable success. Unlike Marsh, Levinstein rarely made images of young muscular or voluptuous bodies, and so the sensuality conveyed by many of his photographs is all the more impressive.

It was only after several years of studying with Grossman and photographing at every possible opportunity that the strong formal and expressive elements began to emerge in Levinstein's photographs. The importance of what he learned in Grossman's class becomes especially clear when one studies the nearly two hundred pages of transcripts of audiotapes of the class that were made in 1950, when Levinstein was a student.[39] Aesthetic notions such as significant form, plastic expression, the relation between positive and negative space expressed in two dimensions, the emotive capacity of abstraction – some of the fundamental concerns of modern painting, ideas one would have expected to hear about in an art class but not in a photography class forty-five years ago – were all discussed in Grossman's classes, and always in relation to the medium of photography. A sampling of his remarks provides a sense of his basic approach:

> The tremendous problem is to discover what material, what area of life is yours. Where does your heart go?
>
> The photographic image replaces naturalistic experience. The question of naturalism is a fallacy, it does not exist . . . Every society produces a way of understanding the nature of appearance and the nature of reality . . . reality is never an absolute.
>
> Only if you have a powerful emotion when you deal with a given object will you understand this design and form in such a way that it is overwhelmingly significant – [so] that you will be able to transform the old way of understanding things into a new way.

38.	In addition to his pen and sketchbook, Marsh sometimes used a 35mm camera as an alternative form of note-taking, especially at Coney Island. His photographs are not very skillfully or deliberately composed — they were clearly meant to be used only as sketches for his painting and printmaking. See Lloyd Goodrich, *Reginald Marsh* (New York: Harry N. Abrams, 1972), p. 40.

39.	David Vestal and Lisette and Evsa Model were among those who attended this class.

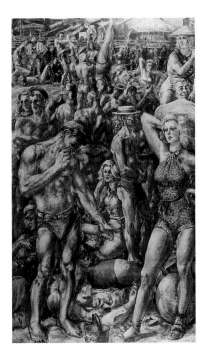

Fig. 11
Ben Shahn
Spring 1947
Tempera on masonite
43.2 × 76.2 cm
Albright-Knox Art Gallery,
Buffalo, N.Y.

Fig. 12
Leon Levinstein
Coney Island 1955
Gelatin silver print
28.0 × 35.6 cm
National Gallery of Canada,
gift of the American Friends
of Canada Committee Inc.,
through the generosity of
Stuart E. Karu
Cat. 14

Fig. 13
Reginald Marsh
Coney Island 1936
Tempera on panel
152.4 × 91.4 cm
Syracuse University Art
Collection, Syracuse, N.Y.

To what extent can you heighten your realistic concept of a natural form in your photographic presentation so that it has more or less abstract qualities? Can you heighten it to the point where it is merely an emotional or plastic equivalent of the object? Could that be one of the final goals that we would be working toward? Is there something in between?[40]

Grossman's greatest impact on Levinstein's artistic development was in the role of teacher. The stylistic influence of Grossman the photographer is generally less pronounced, though it too can be discerned. Beginning in 1945 with the photographs he made in Guatemala and Panama [fig. 14] and continuing in New York in 1947 and 1948 (Coney Island, the San Gennaro Festival in Little Italy), Grossman was doing exactly what he demanded of his students: developing a more personal and dynamic style, moving away from the more straightforward and "objective" manner that had characterized his work in the '30s and early '40s.[41] Unfortunately, there is no telling how Grossman's street work would have evolved over time. Harassed by the FBI, he ceased photographing on the street by the end of 1948. Thus the most creative period of his career, during which the core of his photographic legacy was produced, spanned a period of less than four years.

Grossman did however leave a clue as to the direction his work might have taken. It is couched in a remark that he made to his class in 1950 regarding his excitement about using a 35mm camera. His words presage aspects not only of the work of Levinstein, but of William Klein and Robert Frank as well: "I have finally found an instrument in the small camera – the 35mm camera – toward which I have been working for years . . . which would allow me to do something that is concerned with violence and with energy, and with the firm knowledge which has always been basically instinctive – that there is a violence which comes from the great complexity of our living . . . I cannot be happy with pictures or with material or with an approach to material that tend[s] . . . to give it too clean and too calm a rendition."[42]

In class, Grossman warned his students against imitation, but he often showed and discussed his own photographs, and it is not surprising that Levinstein's photographs would reflect certain aspects of his teacher's work. Grossman was a forceful personality, and Levinstein lacked both self-assurance and an established approach of his own. If there are only a few Levinstein photographs that closely resemble Grossman's, perhaps it is because Levinstein was simply a good student. Rather than imitate his teacher, he assimilated

40.　　Winters transcript. Each quotation is an individual statement taken out of context.

41.　　Grossman had been in Guatemala and Panama as a photographer with the United States Army. For the first time in his life he was free of financial pressures and had little else to do but photograph. Anne Tucker, who has done a great deal of research on Grossman's life, believes that it was this situation which provided him with the opportunity to experiment and redefine himself as a photographer.

42.　　Winters transcript. It is interesting that Grossman was not discussing his photographs of people when he made this statement. The context was a discussion of his remarkable, nearly abstract photographs of seagulls, rocks, and ocean made in Provincetown in 1949.

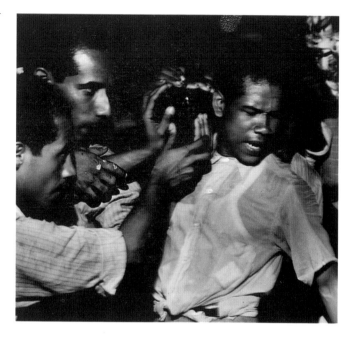

Grossman's ideas and extended certain aspects of his approach. If Grossman came in close on his subjects, Levinstein came in even closer. Where Grossman truncated bodies, eliminating hands and feet in his framing, Levinstein cropped out heads [figs. 15, 16] or filled the frame with a head or a back. Although Levinstein photographed in many of the same places as Grossman, it would be a mistake to interpret this as imitation. A walker and a loner, it was only natural that Levinstein would prowl the streets of New York and the beaches of Coney Island, like numerous other photographers before him. As Levinstein wrote in one of his notebooks, perhaps quoting Grossman, "Influence doesn't mean imitation – influence means feeding and digesting."[43] The process may have taken several years, but by 1952 Levinstein had found his own graphic and direct style.

To many of his students Grossman seemed a gruff and critical person who at times expressed a great deal of bitterness. Yet the energy in Grossman's photographs, especially from the late 1940s, is generally more spirited and engaged than in Levinstein's. Over the years, Levinstein was more concerned with the depiction of solitude, alienation, and struggle; his work is largely concerned with what it takes to live in the city and what the city takes from its inhabitants. Though no seeker after the grotesque or freakish, Levinstein gravitated to the milieu of the outsider, of the person living on the fringes of society.

Levinstein was encouraged by Grossman to look at, study, and read about art and to develop a critical vocabulary.[44] Throughout his life in New York he assiduously visited the city's art galleries and museums. Many of his friends spoke of meeting him at the Museum of Modern Art, where he would spend hours looking at paintings and sculptures as well as photographs.[45] That he kept a notebook is also a testament to Grossman's influence.

Levinstein's notebooks consist primarily of aphorisms or longer statements by photographers, painters, sculptors, and writers on the nature of

43.   Artist's notebook, unpaginated and undated, courtesy of Stuart Karu.

44.   Grossman told his class: "I am suggesting that you do a great deal of research . . . a lot of searching within yourself and a great deal of research in an almost literal sense — studying the work of other photographers, studying anything that has to do with art, every expression of art and every comment on art" (Winters transcript).

45.   Levinstein's taste in art was eclectic, ranging from ancient Chinese bronze sculpture to Haitian folk art, from the Impressionists to Edward Munch to Kenneth Noland. His range was considerably narrower when it came to photography, where he strongly favored the documentary tradition of Atget, Hine, Cartier-Bresson, Walker Evans, Lange, Levitt, and others. His notebooks

Fig. 14
Sid Grossman
Black Christ Festival, Panama
1945
Gelatin silver print
26.1 × 28.6 cm
National Gallery of Canada

Fig. 15
Sid Grossman
Coney Island c. 1947
Gelatin silver print
23.4 × 19.6 cm
National Gallery of Canada

Fig. 16
Leon Levinstein
Untitled c. 1965
Gelatin silver print
28.8 × 26.9 cm
National Gallery of Canada, gift of the American
Friends of Canada Committee, Inc., through the
generosity of Stuart E. Karu
Cat. 54

creativity, the role of the artist in society, what photography is, what photography should be, and so on. He repeatedly quotes Grossman, Cartier-Bresson, and, surprisingly, Edward Weston. Also included are numerous statements identified as being by Berenice Abbott, Walker Evans, Lewis Hine, and Dorothea Lange. There are also unattributed statements, but it is apparent that most of these too are quotations, many presumably from Grossman. Levinstein clearly was trying to formulate his own concept of and approach to photography. It was perhaps out of a sense of inadequacy with language that he felt the need to use the words of others to articulate a position of his own. And a credo of sorts does indeed begin to emerge in the types of statements that are repeated over and over:

> He tries to detail the effects of circumstances on familiar specimens, so that the single face, the single house, the single street strikes with the strength of overwhelming numbers. The terrible cumulative force of thousands of faces, houses, streets. (From an article about Edvard Munch)

> No need for all the elements that reality throws at us. Everything should be clarified. Select the essential.

> Be spontaneous rather than reasoned. Have no method in your work, no deception, no embroidery.

> Must transform your experience and emotion into a picture.

> A picture is an idea made visible on a flat surface.

> Be particular! What you say must be said with passion.

> Shapes should tell you what they are. Shapes should not be an end in themselves. (Grossman)

> The camera must be used for recording life, for rendering the very quintessence of the thing itself. I will let no chance pass to record interesting abstractions, but I feel definite in my belief that the approach to photography is through realism. (Edward Weston)

> Be concerned with expression not representation, creation not imitation. (Paraphrase of a statement by Lisette Model in her letter of reference for Levinstein's Guggenheim Fellowship application for 1967)

> I think to understand better what one sees one has to forget oneself and disappear. (Cartier-Bresson)

> Stare. It is the way to educate your eye, and more. Stare, pry, listen, eavesdrop. Die knowing something. You are not here long. (Walker Evans)

> It is always the instantaneous reaction to oneself that produces a photograph. (Robert Frank)

There is no question that the classes with Grossman were an inspiration and a turning point for Levinstein. As he recalled many years later, "it was a real joy . . . going there because Sid was such a good teacher . . . I lived in Brooklyn then, and I got home once or twice during the summer and it was getting light. And then [I] slept a few hours and went out and photographed the rest of the weekend."[46] Miriam Grossman Cohen

include a poem he wrote in homage to André Kertész and numerous quotations from Cartier-Bresson's introduction to *The Decisive Moment*. However, he was not always predictable. In the mid-1980s Adam Cohen took Levinstein to one of the first New York showings of the Starn Twins. Cohen expected him to dismiss their work as too self-consciously arty, but instead Levinstein came away very impressed (Adam Cohen, from an interview with Adam and Jem Cohen, 25 January 1991).

46.   Levinstein interview.

and several of Grossman's students at the time recall how gratified Grossman felt when Levinstein worked through to his own personal vision in his photographs. As the critic George Wright remarked in his review of Levinstein's 1956 show at Helen Gee's Limelight Gallery: "In an introductory note, he gives credit to the late Sid Grossman, an extraordinary teacher whose influence has been unusually strong on a number of New York photographers. The tribute is graceful and deserved, but Levinstein is standing on his own feet and seeing with his own eyes."[47]

Another photographer who was an important influence on Levinstein in the early stages of his career was Lisette Model. Levinstein was studying with Grossman in 1950 when Lisette and Evsa Model attended the class, and from 1954 until 1960 Levinstein was a student in Evsa Model's painting workshop. As David Vestal remarked, "you couldn't study painting with Evsa without constantly talking with Lisette."[48] Outside of these classes, his social contact with Lisette seems to have been limited to their meeting occasionally at the Limelight, but professionally they were very aware of each other. In interviews, several of Levinstein's friends recalled his appreciation of Model's photography. Model expressed admiration not only for the quality of Levinstein's work, but also for his integrity and commitment to photography.[49]

The most significant lesson that Levinstein gleaned from Model's photographs was how expressive and revealing of one's emotions and inner state of mind the human body could be. From this there followed the realization that the face was just one of many body elements in a portrait, and that in fact a portrait need not include a face. Gestures, posture, the way a person walked or held his hands, all those aspects of an individual's appearance that often go unnoticed, could convey so much about his character and his life [figs. 17, 18]. At times, Levinstein, like Model, was attracted to fleshy, massive bodies, but he did not need a full figure to create images in which the human form, even when compressed into the flat, two-dimensionality of a photograph, projects a sculptural,

47.   George B. Wright, "Levinstein at Limelight: 'Powerful Group of Photos,'" *Village Voice*, 11 January 1956, p. 9.

48.   Vestal interview.

49.   References to his photographs appear several times in her teaching notebooks (Lisette Model Archives, Photographs Collection, National Gallery of Canada).

Fig. 19
Edward Weston
Nude on Sand, Oceano
1936
Gelatin silver print
18.0 × 24.2 cm
National Gallery of Canada,
gift of Dorothy Meigs Eidlitz

Fig. 20
Leon Levinstein
Untitled c. 1960
Gelatin silver print
33.5 × 27.1 cm
National Gallery of Canada

plastic quality. In many of his images, bodies and heads attain a monumental presence, an effect that Levinstein achieved through bold framing and by discovering the dynamic perspective or point of view that would be synergistic with his subject.

Neither Model nor Grossman ever achieved the distillation of form that was to be one of the signature attributes of Levinstein's work. Indeed, in certain of Levinstein's photographs the strength of the forms threatens to overwhelm the content. Yet the images never degenerate into exercises in design or graphic effect. Levinstein was too engaged with his subject matter and too deeply committed to realistic representation for this to occur. Regardless of the degree of abstraction or simplification, the human element is always foremost. As Model noted in a letter of reference she wrote for Levinstein's Guggenheim Fellowship application for 1967: "He creates shapes that have meaning and makes his statement through plastic means and always in relation to life."[50]

Like Model, Levinstein was no purist when it came to achieving a desired result in the final print. Both his mentors, Brodovitch and Grossman, believed that decisions made after the photograph was taken were just as important for the creation of the final work, and they encouraged cropping and manipulation of the image on the negative.[51] Levinstein did not go to the same extremes as Model (such as tilting the printing easel to alter the perspective), but, in addition to cropping, he would sometimes flip the negative in the enlarger. Although it was not unusual for him to crop the square-format negative of the Rolleiflex in order to create a rectangular image, many of his most powerful close-up photographs were made using nearly the entire negative.

At first the connection may seem strained, but it is no accident that many statements from Edward Weston's *Daybooks* are quoted or paraphrased in Levinstein's notebooks. It was not just Weston's lifestyle, commitment, and integrity that Levinstein surely admired, but above all his photography, for in some respects it is the work of Weston that Levinstein's bold handling of photographic form most clearly evokes. The forms in Weston's photographs are generally more defined and more elegant than in Levinstein's. However, Weston's forms are derived from landscapes, still lifes, and compliant models,

50.   Lisette Model, Confidential Report on Candidate for Fellowship, 27 December 1966, Archives of the John Simon Guggenheim Foundation, New York (with permission of the Estate of Lisette Model). Model wrote letters in support of Levinstein's applications for Guggenheim Fellowships for the years 1967, 1968, and 1969. Her letters clearly convey a genuine respect and esteem for Levinstein.

51.   Jane Livingston, *The New York School: Photographs 1936–1963* (New York: Stewart, Tabori and Chang, 1992), p. 296.

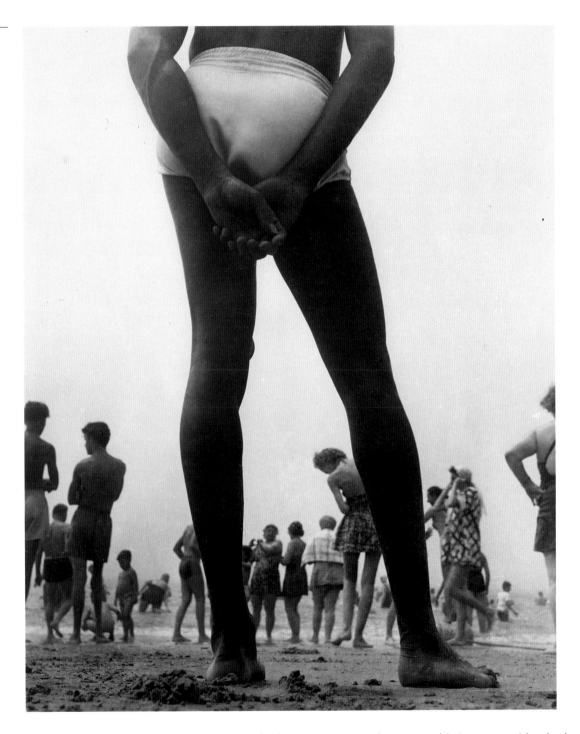

while Levinstein had to maneuver and compose his images amidst the happenstance of streets and everyday life [figs. 19, 20].

Levinstein, a large man, big-boned and over six feet tall, must have spent a great deal of time either crouching, squatting, or kneeling in order to frame not only the subject but also the background and foreground to his satisfaction. In composing his images he was attentive not only to framing but also to the transformation of three-dimensional space into a flat picture plane and to the relationship between the sharp and blurred (out-of-focus or

moving) elements of an image.[52] Like William Klein, he would layer the picture plane to create a feeling of depth or, at times, a very curious, ambiguous sensation of space, simultaneously suggestive of depth and flat two-dimensionality [figs. 21, 22]. Like many photographers with a modernist sensibility, Levinstein often makes one very aware of both the transformation of what he saw into a two-dimensional representation and the image's relationship to what is outside the frame. In some of his photographs the effect is so extreme that he seems to be playing with gravity, at times creating a fluid gesture out of a person's posture [see p. 76]. Of course, Levinstein could not have made the powerful photographs that he did by standing in Times Square or on the beach at Coney Island and stopping to think about composition, or significant form, or any of the things he had learned from painters or from Brodovitch or Grossman. With the various elements of his images –

52.   While discussing a student's work, Sid Grossman once asked his class: "Why do you photograph objects which relate to other objects which relate to other spaces in this area and construct them in this area in certain ways, in given tonalities, in given degrees of focus and given degrees of perspective? Is it purposeful, or to what extent is it purposeful, and why? If there is not a why there has got to be" (Winters transcript).

Fig. 21
Leon Levinstein
Untitled c. 1979
Gelatin silver print
39.3 × 48.8 cm
Stuart E. Karu
Cat. 84

Fig. 22
William Klein
Four Heads, New York 1954
Gelatin silver print
28.9 × 21.7 cm
Courtesy Howard Greenberg
Gallery, New York

bodies and faces – constantly rearranging themselves and appearing and disappearing in the viewfinder, he was forced to make decisions on a more impulsive, intuitive level. As Cartier-Bresson put it, "visual organization can only stem from developed instinct"[53] and "to take photographs means . . . putting one's head, one's eye and one's heart on the same axis."[54]

Levinstein's work quickly began to attract attention. One of his photographs was included in *U.S. Camera Annual 1951*, and two were chosen the following year. In 1956 he was among six featured photographers of the annual, together with Richard Avedon, Wynn Bullock, G.E. Kidder Smith (an architectural photographer), Eugene Smith, and Brett Weston. Over the course of the decade, his work would also be in five *Popular Photography* annuals. In 1952 he was the winner of *Popular Photography*'s international photography contest, with a prize of $2,000 – not a small amount of money at the time. (As a point of comparison, a Guggenheim Fellowship in photography then amounted to $3,000.) Given *Popular Photography*'s penchant for trying to appeal to both an amateur and professional audience in those years, it is not surprising that the winning picture, titled *Boys*, a close-up of three black children,[55] was considered by several of his photographer friends to be the most sentimental of those that Levinstein had submitted.

It is important to maintain some perspective on the situation of photographers in the 1950s who were neither photojournalists nor commercial photographers. Although magazines such as *Popular Photography* and *U.S. Camera Annual* may, to some extent, have represented "the jukebox level of American taste,"[56] there were precious few

53.   Henri Cartier-Bresson, in his introduction to *The Decisive Moment* (New York: Simon and Schuster, 1952).

54.   Quoted in Paul Hill and Thomas Cooper, *Dialogue with Photography* (New York: Farrar Strauss Giroux, 1979), p. 76.

55.   *Popular Photography*, December 1952, p. 61.

56.   Minor White, quoted in Jonathan Green, *American Photography: A Critical History / 1945 to the Present* (New York: Harry N. Abrams, 1984), p. 70.

Fig. 23
Leon Levinstein
Untitled 1954
Gelatin silver print
41.9 × 38.9 cm
Stuart E. Karu
Cat. 12

alternatives for the publication of photography as art.[57] At the time, they were certainly the most influential and accessible channels for creative photographers. The magazine *Aperture*, which was founded in 1952 and presented serious critical writing as well as reproductions of photographs, eventually came to have a very strong influence on those photographers, curators, and writers who viewed photography as a means of personal and artistic expression. In the 1950s, however, it was hardly known outside of a very small circle of subscribers (approximately 300 in the mid-1950s). Perhaps that is why Robert Frank, Lisette Model, and Gary Winogrand were among those also submitting their photographs to these photography magazines and annuals.

Opportunities for exhibiting serious photographs were also quite limited. The only museums that were consistently organizing photography exhibitions in the 1950s were the Museum of Modern Art in New York, the Art Institute of Chicago, and the George Eastman House in Rochester, New York. However, the director of the Department of Photography at the Museum of Modern Art, Edward Steichen, was very receptive to young photographers, especially in the early '50s, and it was fairly easy to get an appointment with him to show one's portfolio.

From the very outset, Steichen was clearly impressed with Levinstein's photographs, and he was to be a life-long supporter.[58] In addition to purchasing prints and writing letters of support for two of Levinstein's Guggenheim Fellowship applications, Steichen included his work in seven exhibitions over a period of a decade, beginning in 1952 with the exhibition *Then and Now* and including the immensely popular *Family of Man* [fig. 23]. In the 1953 exhibition *Always the Young Strangers*, Levinstein's pictures were shown alongside works by several other relatively unknown photographers; this, however, was an exception. In the other exhibitions organized by Steichen, such as *Seventy Photographers Look at New York* and *Contemporary American Photography* (the American component of *The Exhibition of Contemporary Photography*), Levinstein was included with photographers of the stature of Berenice Abbott, Harry Callahan, Walker Evans, Helen Levitt, Lisette Model, Aaron Siskind, and Eugene Smith.

Steichen once noted that Levinstein was one of the few photographers who had so much material suitable for *The Family of Man*,[59] yet many of the Levinstein photographs that he chose to show or purchase were not typical of the humanistic, sometimes sentimental imagery that he promoted in that exhibition. He was quick to identify and appreciate the strong formal element in Levinstein's work, as well as Levinstein's inclination to confront and document some of the harsher aspects of life in New York. This was especially true in the mid-to-late 1950s, when Levinstein was maturing as a photographer and his style becoming more defined.

The other important supporter of Levinstein's work throughout most of his career was Helen Gee, the founder of the Limelight Gallery, the first American gallery devoted

57.   Referring to those years, William Klein has stated: "Fashion magazines were our art magazines" (Livingston, p. 265.).

58.   Levinstein's friend Leon Schnall tells a story about introducing Levinstein's work to Steichen. Schnall kept encouraging Levinstein to take his photographs to Steichen, but he kept putting it off. One day Schnall went up to Levinstein's office at Colby Advertising to meet him for lunch, and when he got there Levinstein was busy in a meeting. Noticing a pile of photographs on the desk, Schnall stuffed them into a portfolio and dropped them off with Steichen's secretary. The next day, Levinstein, who had not noticed that the prints were missing amidst the clutter of his desk, got a call from Steichen saying he wanted to purchase some prints for the collection. Levinstein did not at first believe that it was really Steichen calling (Schnall interview).

59.   Edward Steichen, 1955, Confidential Report on Candidate for Fellowship, Archives of the John Simon Guggenheim Foundation, New York.

solely to the exhibition and sale of photographs. The Limelight, which was in existence from 1954 to 1961, was located near Sheridan Square in New York's Greenwich Village. The gallery was in a separate space at the rear of what turned out to be a very popular coffeehouse. This arrangement served to ensure its financial stability, in a time when selling two prints from a show was considered a success and the average price of a print was $30. The Limelight was a completely professional endeavor – from the care taken in the hanging of the shows to the announcements and press previews that were arranged for each exhibition. Most important, though, was the quality of the work shown. In the seven years that the Limelight was open, Helen Gee mounted more than sixty exhibitions, including work by Berenice Abbott, Bill Brandt, Imogene Cunningham, Robert Frank, Lisette Model, Aaron Siskind, Eugene Smith, Paul Strand, Edward Weston, and Minor White, as well as work by historical figures such as Eugène Atget and Julia Margaret Cameron.

In 1955 Levinstein's work was included in a summer group exhibition, which was the way Gee usually presented the work of younger or lesser known photographers. The following January she gave him a one-person show. Gee recalls that the show created a lot of excitement and a few prints were even sold.[60] There were favorable reviews by Jacob Deschin in the *New York Times* and George Wright in *The Village Voice*. Wright's review begins: "The current exhibit at Limelight really opens the year on a strong note. The selection of over 80 photographs by Leon Levinstein is a powerful group of pictures by a photographer whose work is too rarely seen." He continues: "Levinstein has a remarkable sense of form and his prints are beautifully and strongly structured, with every element within the rectangle working for him."[61] Gee included Levinstein in another group show in 1959. She also tried to promote his work and to introduce him to other people who might be able to further his career. In at least one instance, Levinstein demonstrated what Gee considered his "will to fail," or fear of success, by not showing up for an interview she had arranged for him with John English, the influential art director at *McCall's*.[62] Nonetheless, Gee remained a loyal supporter, and in 1980 she included his work in the exhibition *Photography of the Fifties*, a major retrospective that she organized for the Center for Creative Photography in Tucson (which also resulted in the purchase of nine prints by the Center). The following year she was instrumental in arranging the sale of a substantial number of prints to the art dealer Harry Lunn.

The Limelight was important not just as a showcase for photography, but also as a meeting place for New York photographers, professional and nonprofessional alike. Roy DeCarava, Louis Faurer, Robert Frank, Lisette Model, and Eugene Smith were among the regular frequenters of its coffeehouse. For Levinstein the Limelight was the mainstay of his very limited social life. He would hang out there with the Models and with other former students of Sid Grossman such as Ray Jacobs, Harry Lapow, Victor Obsatz, and David Vestal.

60.   Interview with Helen Gee, 10 February 1992.

61.   Wright, p. 63.

62.   Gee interview.

Levinstein left Colby Advertising in 1953 and apparently did not take a full-time position again until 1968, when he went to work as an art director for Brown & Gravenson, a catalogue merchandising firm based in New York. During the intervening fifteen years he listed his occupation as self-employed photographer, though it seems that he in fact earned most of his income as a freelance graphic designer and art director, working seasonally on catalogues, and only occasionally taking on commercial photography assignments. Whatever the case may have been, it is clear that at this point in his life he had decided to commit himself to his personal work in photography rather than further his career in advertising.

From about 1956 until 1960 he shared a studio, located at 32nd Street near Lexington Avenue, with a commercial photographer, Sam Meinhold. According to Arthur Porta, Meinhold's assistant at the time, Levinstein had no patience for the exacting work of studio photography. When he did attempt to set up a shot in the studio, he was "all thumbs" and totally disorganized. He seems to have been interested in the studio primarily for the use of the darkroom.[63] Porta vividly recalls the sight of Levinstein's hands and clothes stained with fixer and covered with cigarette ash as he emerged from the darkroom. More than a few of his prints also emerged this way.[64]

Although he photographed some ads for pharmaceutical companies, Levinstein did most of his work as a commercial photographer for one client, the Doremus Agency, which specialized in advertising and public relations for banks, insurance companies, and other financial institutions [fig. 24].[65] More comfortable out of the studio, Levinstein almost always worked on location, shooting ads with models and also doing portraits of bank and corporation executives in their offices. In the early '60s, Larry Siegel, who at the time ran Image Gallery, a semi-cooperative photography gallery on East 10th Street, assisted Levinstein on some assignments. He remembers one job at a construction site where Levinstein ambled about, utterly oblivious to the hazardous surroundings, his eye never raised from the viewfinder of his Rolleiflex.[66]

Levinstein was not very successful as a commercial photographer, and there are several plausible explanations for this, beginning with his impatience and lack of technical expertise. Feeling that commercial work might encroach on his personal photographic work, he never really pursued it with the degree of intensity that was, and still is, required to be a successful freelance photographer in New York. Finally, as Arthur Porta noted, it was evident that he did not understand the "diplomacy" of doing business. It was the same lack of diplomacy that seems to have marred some of his relationships with dealers and galleries later in his life.

Everyone who knew him described Levinstein as a solitary person. Yet many of those who portrayed him in this way also thought of him as a close friend. They had known him for fifteen, twenty, and in some cases more than thirty years. His friendship with the

63.   Levinstein generally used his apartment bathroom as a darkroom for developing film, but it would have been extremely awkward to make his 14 × 17 and 16 × 20 inch prints — large for that time — under such conditions.
64.   Interview with Arthur Porta, 11 February 1992.
65.   Schnall interview.
66.   Interview with Larry Siegel, 15 January 1992.

"A HELPING HAND" BY LEON LEVINSTEIN

SO SECURITY CAN BEGIN AT ANY AGE...

Equitable's <u>Living</u> Insurance pays off for the <u>living</u>

Living Insurance means benefits for the living. Benefits for you while you live. If you die, benefits for those who live on after you.

A child is born. Your challenge from the very first week: to give her all the protection you can. You can start *today* to assure her, your wife and yourself, security over the years.

Living Insurance Family Style provides up to $15,000 on Dad as basic protection for his family. And you get, in the same low-cost package: coverage for Mom and each insured child. Future children, too, are protected at no extra cost. (Starting when they're

at least 14 days old.) You can choose from: (1) A Family Protection plan which features immediate protection but also has growing cash values. (2) A Family Security plan which emphasizes the savings feature.

This is just one example of *Living* Insurance in action. Ask your Man from Equitable about other forms that can help you send your child to college, protect your home, or meet major medical bills. *The Equitable Life Assurance Society of the U. S., 393 Seventh Avenue, New York 1, N. Y.*

Living Insurance by Equitable

Fig. 24
Leon Levinstein
Advertisement for Equitable
Insurance Company, n.d.

photographer Ray Jacobs and his wife Eleanor was typical. They met Levinstein in the early '50s and quickly became friends; Ray was a student of Sid Grossman's and Eleanor frequently sat in on the classes. Every Friday night they would meet at a Seventh Avenue coffee shop for a hamburger before class. After Levinstein stopped attending Grossman's classes, they continued to see each other frequently because both Leon and Eleanor were studying painting with Evsa Model. Levinstein would sometimes come over for dinner, and occasionally he would accompany Ray to a jazz club late at night. By the early '60s, when Levinstein had stopped attending Evsa Model's painting workshop, they saw him only occasionally – perhaps once or twice a year, and even less frequently in the last fifteen years of his life.[67] In interview after interview with old friends and colleagues the comment was virtually the same: "Leon was a dear and close friend, but, you know, I never saw him that much." Often the contact would consist of nothing more than chance meetings on the street or at the Museum of Modern Art and going to sit with him for an hour over a cup of coffee. Somehow that was enough to nurture some very warm feelings for the man, feelings that could be sustained for twenty or thirty years.

Besides leading a solitary life, Levinstein was also a very private person. He was never forthcoming about his family or his early years. As Eleanor Jacobs remarked: "We knew nothing about him, and we were close friends!"[68] Friends didn't know about other friends, and his family knew nothing about his life in New York except that he made his living as a graphic artist in advertising, that he walked the streets of New York taking pictures, and that, as his sister noted, "he seemed to find himself in New York."[69] When three of his photographs were included in *The Family of Man*, he was very briefly a celebrity in the family. In general, though, they did not follow his photographic career.

From the time he left Baltimore, Levinstein had very little contact with his family. His younger brother Eli had died of cancer in 1936 at the age of twenty-four, and his father died in May 1946, just about the time Leon left for New York. He visited his mother infrequently, and he never got along with his older brother; after their mother's death in 1963, he never saw or spoke to him again. He also rarely saw his sister Bernice. This changed somewhat in the late '70s and early '80s, when he was frequently traveling abroad to photograph. Upon returning to the United States, he would stay in her Baltimore apartment for a few days or a week, resting and reading his mail, which had been forwarded to her while he was away. Levinstein was often a very critical and contentious guest, unappreciative of his sister's hospitality and straining her affection. His visits were not especially pleasant for either of them. Yet Levinstein kept returning, apparently needing the human contact and familial connection that he spent most of his life rejecting.

Not surprisingly, he had little success in his relations with women. Some women saw him as "a perfect gentleman," while others were said to have found him abrasive. Several old friends recall him dating a number of different women in the late '40s and early '50s but never becoming seriously involved. In the mid-'50s he started seeing a young woman who worked with him at Colby Advertising. It seems that she rejected him when he

67.   Jacobs interview.

68.   Ibid.

69.   Interview with Bernice Karu, 18 November 1992.

began to get serious, and a short time later she married another man.[70] After this episode he shied away from any intimate relationships.

The pain of an unrequited love may have convinced him to forgo any further attempts at personal intimacy, but Levinstein's discomfort in social situations and his avoidance of emotional attachments were evident from childhood. If being an outsider was part of his nature, it was also something that he saw as necessary to his work: "You have got to be alone and work alone, and it's a lonely occupation, if you want to call it that."[71]

Whatever psychic armor Levinstein felt the need for in personal relationships was not in evidence when he photographed. One tends to think of photographing as an emotionally safe activity, the camera acting as a shield, distancing the photographer from his situation or surroundings. However, "playing it safe" is one phrase that does not apply to Levinstein's work. Many of his photographs in fact speak to us of emotional and sometimes even physical risk.[72] He didn't censor himself, and he didn't look away. "Anything that comes within my sight or in my path that excites me to photograph, I'll photograph."[73] More than any technique, it is this immediacy, this excitement in the act of photographing, that creates the emotional intensity and remarkable sense of physicality in many of his images. His mentor Sid Grossman had taught that true photography was not about searching for truth or creating art, but was rather "an act of living . . . a way of passionately dealing with the most intimate material."[74] Leon Levinstein pursued photography with that level of involvement and commitment.

Though many of his street portraits bear witness to a deep understanding of isolation and loneliness, his own solitariness did not deter him from portraying scenes of intimacy or of the longing for human connection. On the contrary, it seems to have sensitized him to these moments and exchanges, much as the absence of physical intimacy in his life may have contributed to the charged energy that radiates from many of his photographs. The images range from tender embraces between couples or parent and child[75] to interactions between the sexes that are sometimes humorous, but more often sad, desperate, and almost grotesque in their absence of any sign of warmth or genuine relatedness. Many of these encounters between the sexes are confined to looking – whether mutual or guardedly one-sided. In some of these photographs, Levinstein portrays the aggressiveness of the male gaze while apparently acknowledging his own voyeurism as well. Often there is a feeling that real intimacy is not likely to be achieved and that the figures are entrapped in a rather sad human drama.

In terms of exhibitions and recognition, the '50s were the high point of Levinstein's career. After 1960 he would not be in any exhibitions until 1964, when John Szarkowski, Steichen's successor at the Museum of Modern Art, included one of Levinstein's most striking images from Coney Island [see p. 62] in the exhibition and book *The Photographer's*

70.   Schnall and Grossman Cohen interviews.

71.   Levinstein interview.

72.   Several times in the 1988 interview by Adam and Jem Cohen, Levinstein responds to questions about his photographs by talking about a particular risk or threat of physical harm that he experienced while he was photographing.

73.   Artist's statement for Guggenheim Fellowship application for 1975, Archives of the John Simon Guggenheim Foundation, New York.

74.   Winters transcript.

75.   Several friends noted that, although he never expressed it in words, Levinstein clearly loved children and seemed to regret not having a family of his own.

Eye. Such was the pattern through the '60s and into the '70s – usually just one or two photographs included in large group exhibitions. These were: *About New York, Night and Day, 1915–1965* at the Gallery of Modern Art in 1965, *The Camera as Witness* at Montreal's Expo 67 [see p. 72], *Harlem on My Mind* at the Metropolitan Museum of Art in 1969, and *The Jew in New York* at the Midtown Y Gallery in 1973.[76]

There are several reasons why Levinstein's work was being exhibited less through the '60s and '70s. By 1963 the two chief supporters of his work were no longer involved in exhibiting photography in New York. Helen Gee closed the Limelight Gallery in 1961, and in 1963 Edward Steichen retired as director of the Department of Photography at the Museum of Modern Art. Unlike Robert Frank and William Klein, Levinstein never had a monograph of his photographs published, and the little commercial photography that he was doing was not the high-profile type of work that would have kept his name current, as with the fashion photography of Richard Avedon or the editorial work of Diane Arbus and Bruce Davidson. Levinstein did not benefit from the rising popularity of photography as an art form, a phenomenon that began in the mid-1970s. Mistrustful of most curators and dealers and uncomfortable with the art scene in general, Levinstein was unwilling or unable to promote himself. Many of his old friends insist that he was not the least bit interested in success, but there is good reason to believe that success, at least in terms of recognition, was indeed very important to him. By the mid-1950s Levinstein had developed what David Vestal saw as a "touchy self-respect" – he had a sense of himself as a talented and important photographer, yet he was nagged by a constant feeling of insecurity and fear of rejection.[77] In at least one instance in the early '80s, he became enraged at a curator's noncommittal response to his work.[78] However, his relationships with curators and photography dealers were not all negative. Several dealers and curators have described him as easy to work with and appreciative of the attention. One curator enjoyed dealing with him specifically because she felt that he was not angry and bitter like some other older photographers who had not received much recognition.[79]

Another important factor working against Levinstein's career was the changing nature of photography itself, both in terms of aesthetics and the attitudes of photographers. By the mid-1960s in America, all aspects of the photography that was exhibited and considered as art were beginning to undergo a transformation, one which would continue and accelerate over the next two decades. While some photographers were pushing the limits of the modernist tradition, others were questioning the assumptions of this tradition and experimenting with subject matter, technique, and the appearance of the photographic image. Documentary photography had lost its prominence and was the target of increasing skepticism as to its ability to represent and interpret the world. Street photography, for those such as Lee Friedlander [fig. 25] or Gary Winogrand who still photographed on the street, was a practice with very different concerns than those of previous decades. The mastery of formal subtleties combined with an ironic and disengaged relation to subject were what characterized most of the street photography of the 1960s and '70s. Levinstein was one of the few street photographers who did not burn out after a decade or so, and the quality and impact of the photographs he produced over the years did not diminish. But

76.   Levinstein did have six or seven photographs in *The Jew in New York*, organized by Larry Siegel. However, over thirty photographers were included, with more than two hundred prints in the exhibition (Siegel interview).

77.   Vestal interview.

78.   Grossman Cohen interview.

79.   Conversation with Susan Kismaric, February 1991.

Fig. 25
Lee Friedlander
Paris 1978
Gelatin silver print
35.5 × 42.9 cm
National Gallery of Canada

Fig. 26
Leon Levinstein
Untitled 1970s
Gelatin silver print
35.4 × 28.3 cm
Stuart E. Karu

because his basic approach and style did not change, his work was strongly identified with an earlier decade. It is unfortunate but not surprising that just as photography was coming to be recognized and appreciated as an art form by a greater audience than ever before, Levinstein's work was being ignored and for the most part forgotten.

Leon Levinstein walked and photographed – the two activities were virtually inseparable for him – in the streets of New York over a period of more than thirty years. Although he travelled a great deal and photographed in Europe, Mexico, Haiti, and India, the overwhelming majority of his best images were made in certain neighborhoods of New York to which he would return week after week, year after year: Coney Island, the Lower East Side, Midtown around Fifth Avenue, and Times Square. He chose these parts of the city (as well as Harlem in the 1950s) because of the activity on the streets.[80] As he told Helen Gee, he went "where the life is."[81] Over the years these neighborhoods were changing, mostly deteriorating, and often leaving very little of the street life that had drawn him there in the first place. Entire sections of the Lower East Side were torn down and replaced with monolithic high-rise housing projects. Other parts of this impoverished but once vibrant neighborhood were left to decay even further, and the streets were abandoned to muggers and junkies; people stayed in their apartments and watched television. All this he found lamentable but not surprising. "Nothing in New York changes for the better," he remarked.[82]

Although generally quiet and reserved, Levinstein could be very argumentative and out-spoken in his opinions about art and politics. His artistic likes and dislikes and his political views were expressed most vociferously in heated discussions with friends, especially his close friend Harry Lapow.[83] Several people have described Levinstein as being firmly liberal in his political beliefs, but not in any sense activist, and politics did not play a direct or significant role in his photography. Levinstein always insisted that he did not have any "agenda" when he photographed and that he never tried to make a specific statement with his work. In his proposal for a Guggenheim Fellowship for the year 1975 he wrote: "I prefer to work without any specific idea in mind." His only mandate, he felt, was "to make the energy and particular quality that I feel in American life a part of my photography."[84] However, working without an agenda did not prevent him from making, if only incidentally, some very pointed observations in his photographs about social and political realities. Because he was more interested in the

80. Speaking about his early days photographing on the streets, he said: "Of course on Park Avenue you never did see women . . . looking out the window gossiping with neighbors . . . [There was] no feeling of family at all that you could reach. So you went into the neighborhoods like the Lower East Side or Harlem . . . and people accepted you even if you were taking their picture" (Levinstein interview).

81. Helen Gee, "Where the Life Is," *Camera Arts*, March/April 1982, p. 50.

82. Levinstein interview.

83. Interview with Gary Lapow, 12 December 1991.

84. Artist's statement for Guggenheim Fellowship application for 1975, Archives of the John Simon Guggenheim Foundation, New York.

personal drama than the social context, and because his tight framing often reduced context to a minimum, these observations are often muted.

In the mid-1960s Levinstein was photographing a great deal in the area around Times Square. It was then that he began to work mainly with the Leica, a compact and quiet 35mm camera that he had obtained in the late '50s or early '60s. Although he would continue to use the Rolleiflex, most of the photographs from the last two decades of his career were made with the Leica. One reason for the change was the desire to work more quickly and attract less attention in a neighbourhood such as Times Square. In addition, the Leica afforded him an opportunity to explore color as he began shooting 35mm slides.

In his application for a Guggenheim Fellowship for 1967 Levinstein stated: "For the past year I have been experimenting with color in the straight documentary style, trying to use color as an added expressive dimension and always in terms of the medium – wanting only the stark realism the lens can so exactly render, presented without interference of 'artistic effect.'"[85] It was only shortly before his death that he acknowledged another, more mundane reason for shooting color slides then: he had grown tired of working in the darkroom. Oddly, there are no color prints from the slides that he shot in Times Square, but there are at least half a dozen black-and-white photographs that he printed from conversion negatives made from the slides. These images, as well as most of the color slides dating from this period, are stylistically indistinguishable from his other work. Hardly anyone knew that he had photographed in color. Patrick Pagnano, a younger street photographer who became friends with him in the mid-1970s, recalled that he was always afraid of showing his work to Levinstein because of the adamancy with which he dismissed color photography.[86] Although he abandoned shooting in color in the Times Square area after a year or two, that locale, never short on street life, would continue to attract him for at least another decade.[87]

No photographer could be faulted for a projecting a harsh image of street life in New York in recent decades. However, by the 1970s, it is an especially bleak view of the city and its people that prevails in Levinstein's photographs [fig. 26]. At times, an atmosphere of desperation or violence seems to permeate the work, and the photographer, no stranger to solitude, seems to depict it more and more frequently in his photographs.

85.   Artist's statement for Guggenheim Fellowship application for 1967, Archives of the John Simon Guggenheim Foundation, New York.

86.   Interview with Patrick Pagnano, 4 November 1991.

87.   The only other color photography that he did was during his travels, mainly in India in the late '70s and early '80s, but even then he was still working primarily in black-and-white.

To what extent this emphasis is a reflection of the photographer's state of mind and to what degree it mirrors the very real decline of the city is difficult to say. What is clear is that during the last fifteen years that he photographed, Levinstein produced a stark and somber document of the daily struggle to survive in the city, both economically and spiritually. Yet he never portrayed his subjects as victims. His photographs do not sentimentalize or heroicize. His response to the world, as recorded in his photographs, seems to have been a mixture of fascination, amusement, sadness, and compassion – and always a basic acceptance of people as they are. He chose to witness and portray, with unflinching honesty, people and situations that most of us would avert our eyes from and quickly pass by – to witness but not to judge. The bitterness and frustration that Levinstein sometimes felt during these years may partly account for the grim view of the city in these later images, but no candid New Yorker would deny that this is what the city can look and feel like on any given day.

During the late '70s and into the '80s many people lost track of Levinstein. He was frequently traveling and for several years did not have an apartment in New York but stayed in inexpensive hotels and short-term sublets, or occasionally with a friend. Among the people he kept in touch with were his old friend Leon Schnall, the photographers Sy Kattelson, Patrick Pagnano, and Bruce Gilden, and Helen Gee, who continued to work with photography as a writer, consultant, and guest curator. He also renewed his friendship with Miriam Grossman Cohen and her family. Her two sons, Adam and Jem, were very close to him in his last years and did whatever they could to promote his work.

The last decade of Levinstein's life was a mixture of frustrating disappointments and belated recognition. A portfolio financed by the art dealer Harry Lunn was printed but never marketed.[88] A one-person exhibition at Photograph Gallery in 1982 never happened – the gallery folded. An exhibition at Light Gallery did take place in the summer of 1982, but at the time the gallery was apparently undergoing financial difficulties and was often closed to the public.[89] Towards the very end, Levinstein was extremely bitter about how little he had managed to earn – whether in appreciation or wealth – from forty years of dedication to photography. He confided to several friends, including Kattelson and Pagnano, that he regretted not having put more time and energy into furthering his career in advertising. From his hospital bed a few days before his death, he counseled Pagnano not to let his son become a photographer.

On the positive side, Harry Lunn did purchase a large group of Levinstein's photographs, and his work was being included in important exhibitions of postwar documentary photography, beginning in 1978 with *New Standpoints* at the Museum of Modern Art. In 1980 there was the exhibition organized by Helen Gee, *Photography of the Fifties*. This was followed by *American Images* at the Barbican Art Gallery in London and *The New York School* at the Corcoran Gallery in Washington, both in 1985. Since his death

88.   There were apparently several reasons why the portfolios were not sold. The most concrete one was that Levinstein ruined many of the excellent prints (made by Sid Kaplan) by sloppy spotting.

89.   Just a few years before his death, Levinstein rejected the offer of another important New York photography gallery to represent him. He stated at the time that his association with the gallery would complicate an impending sale of prints to a museum, even though the gallery was willing to stay out of the transaction (conversation with Howard Greenberg, March 1993).

in 1988 his work has received more notice and has continued to be exhibited. Although still not widely known, Levinstein has gradually come to be acknowledged as a key figure from a very significant era of American photography.

From 1978 until 1985 Levinstein was travelling a great deal, often at a pace that would have been challenging for a person even half his age. Beginning in October 1982 he was on the road for an entire year – in Europe, North Africa, India, Nepal, and back to Europe – often staying in cheap hotels and traveling by bus or train. It is apparent from the journals he kept (they are more like logs than personal diaries) that these trips were far from being vacations. Although he did not overlook the standard attractions of museums, churches, and temples, he spent most of his time walking the streets and photographing, just as he liked to do in New York.[90] And the success or failure of each day was judged in terms of the pictures: "Monday, March 22 – Went to Bhaktapur. Maybe a couple of fair shots. Not doing too well. Can't get that one shot. Supper of vegetables at hotel. Should leave Thursday."[91]

Levinstein remained vigorous and in reasonably good health until 1985, when he was hit by a car on the streets of New York. He wasn't seriously injured, but he never fully regained his mobility. He had to curtail his walking, and he no longer carried his cameras with him. Several friends recall that they first became aware of his age – he was seventy-five years old – after the accident. A few years later he was injured again, kicked in the head while struggling with a mugger in the elevator of his Bronx apartment building. He died of a stroke in December 1988.

There is a stylistic distinction made in regard to documentary photographers, especially street photographers, between those who acknowledge their subject and make their presence known and those who prefer to work furtively, with their subjects unaware. All of the photographers who knew Levinstein remarked on his uncanny ability to go unnoticed in the middle of a crowd or in the midst of a tense situation and photograph unobtrusively. Levinstein would set out from his apartment, or his office at lunchtime, in a tie and jacket and wearing a hat or cap, regardless of the season. He walked with his Leica in the palm of his large hand, the strap wrapped around his wrist, and the Rolleiflex cradled in the crook of his arm. He worked quickly and deliberately, often without a light meter and with his camera focus preset, so as to avoid any unnecessary activity that might arouse attention. "Look like a tourist" was the advice he gave to younger photographers.[92]

90.   Levinstein was especially captivated by India and told several friends that being there was one of the high points of his life. He first visited India in the '60s, and he returned several times in the late '70s and early '80s. He always travelled alone, though he would sometimes link up briefly with other westerners he would meet in hotels or restaurants. Probably feeling at home in its crowded and vibrant streets, he shot hundreds of rolls of film in India, mostly black-and-white but also some color slides. He apparently made no color prints from the slides, and from the thousands of black-and-white negatives, he produced only a handful of powerful images of Indian street life. The dozens of other prints from India, even when quite wrenching, display a cultural and emotional distance that one rarely finds in his work. In some of the photographs he seems to have been overwhelmed or seduced by cultural difference; others, perhaps as a result of attempting to avoid just such a seduction, seem uncharacteristically flat.

91.   Personal journals, unpaginated, and undated as to year, courtesy of Stuart Karu.

92.   I am grateful to Douglas Fraser and Allen Hochman for providing this description. They would sometime accompany Levinstein on his lunchtime photographic forays to the Times Square area when all three worked for Brown & Gravenson in the late '60s and early '70s.

Yet, paradoxically, Levinstein is nearly always a presence in his photographs. Unlike certain photographers whose work leaves one with the feeling that the photographer and you, the viewer, have come across the image in the photograph quite by chance, Levinstein constantly draws attention to himself, forcing you to acknowledge the choices he made. His presence is felt not only in his selection of subject, but also in his framing and point of view. It is as though he were not only saying "Look at what I saw!" but also insisting that we look at the world as he saw and felt it. With work as subjective and emotionally engaging as Levinstein's, we soon come to realize that this man, who in life shared his intimate self with no one, stands transparent before us, revealed in his photographs.

MAX KOZLOFF

Leon Levinstein
and the School of New York

The photographer Leon Levinstein died in 1988. He had been only mildly noticed during his time, led a narrow life, and seems to have had but few friends. Some of them, who knew the depth of his work, were concerned that it should be remembered, for at his death at age 78, Levinstein's street photography had long been out of fashion. He became a member of the New York school only after it had peaked in the '40s and '50s. Levinstein was centered in the tough-minded pictorial mode practiced by such other loners as Weegee and Lisette Model, and even Ben Shahn, when that painter photographed in the Depression. Toward the end, Levinstein complained that the professional atmosphere had become too intellectual, by which he meant detached and unfeeling. These words may be too bland to suggest his real attitude toward a scene into which he was reluctant to fit. "He slammed shut every door that opened," wrote Helen Gee, who knew him well enough, "and the dismal thought once crossed my mind that success would come to Levinstein . . . once he was no longer around to stand in its way."

The pictures that he left are unsorted. He invariably stamped or signed them, with a particularly aggressive and jagged signature. But they lack captions and dates, omissions that were certainly deliberate. It was as if he would not bring order to his career nor specify the places he had been. The images justified themselves on their own terms, or they did not.

Unlike some colleagues, he was affected by a retrospective mood even as he was immersed in the excitements of the present. It was not any one class of subject, but the modernist sensibility to which his work looks back. At the same time, there is something home-made about this modernism; it protests itself all the more as the visual interest is caught up with something as apparently trivial as a momentary impression of a face. One feels that the photographer constantly searches for a kind of shallow space which a head, limbs, or a figure will dominate, as if each were a kind of monument. Modernism, here, means a tightening of the forces within the field, achieved through effects of design. Levinstein earned his living as a layout man for commercial catalogues. Perhaps he believed that the real life with which he was concerned in photography had to be laid out, too, with high discipline, so that it could testify to his seriousness. Certainly he cut into his images and radically cropped them, in ceaseless study of the arrangements that were possible in his unpremeditated or opportunistic approach to people on the street. The square format of the Rolleiflex camera he used in the '50s appears to have been only a point of departure for prints that wound up as oblongs or verticals, even panoramas. Concision of framing was always linked with intimacy of contact. So, Levinstein retroactively worked back into his original framing, to inform it with a kind of tension which he could not necessarily organize first time around in the heat and the chaos of the photographic moment.

Yet, his work often is ignited and depends upon an encounter with strong emotions. In an interview conducted by Adam and Jem Cohen, the photographer speaks on one hand of his unreflective, instinctual program and yet of the discreet behavior necessary for him to stalk potential subjects. He would not interfere with their reality, lest it be disturbed or reduced in liveliness by consciousness of his presence. Over and over, pictures by Levinstein imply either his miraculous invisibility or the timely distraction of those he photographed. (The twin-lens reflex allowed him to point his camera sideways, while facing away from the motif and looking *down*. It was a strategy that he thought permitted him to maneuver into point blank range without causing suspicion.) Certainly he brings us impossibly close into the personal territory of others and redefines it as one we share with them without any right of entry. It is not a social space; and however intrusive, it is not even much of a narrative or a knowingly psychological space. He did not think he was eavesdropping in what, for him, was a public area. The more one looks, the more one unexpectedly comes to think of it as a zone for still life, made unaccountably vibrant and combustible by its human content.

If his New Yorkers often have a prepossessing bulk, it's not always because they were fat; he liked volume and sought it out from vantages that emphasized unusual or even unrecognizable shapes within the frame. A reclining man's dark raised elbows are seen as if by an ant on the beach. A speaker on some podium is looked at from behind and below so that his silhouette resembles that of a humped beast, with a tie/tail dangling in front. All this strikes one as very energetic and socially unassuming. It appears to be the work of a picture maker for whom discovered relationships between shapes and voids ideally precede those between subjects among themselves. Whether the people he photographed were at rest or in frenetic action, at the edge of blur, a reductive formal intelligence stamps itself upon the scene. Much of the urban setting and people's clothes are steamed out of the depth of field, a reason why Levinstein's work gives us little period flavor. One senses a determined ego, shy sometimes at the moment of exposure, and also a relentless, scouring eye fixated on gesture, face, or other vignettes of body language described at the expense of place.

For all that, Levinstein's jolting approach and the raunchy world reported in these photographs, if only by implication, is very local, unmistakably New York. He was drawn to everything vernacular and licentious that rose up in the sheer ethnic, have-not magnitude of the city. How people made out with each other, and what their life on the streets or bad diets did to age them – their loud styles and sour expressions, distrust, resignation, boredom, ecstasy: such was his meat. He seems to have made a series on the circus. Coney Island was one of his favorite prowls, like that of so many other New York photographers. Nor did he ignore drug culture, prostitution, the Easter parade, and Hasidim in the park. A fair number of his people seem to be arguing; others hang around. Older and fleshy subjects prevail over children. The light beats down harshly on the faces in the crowd, or else they are cast in shadow – there's little tolerance for midtones in this almost tropical world of stone and pavement. Forty-Second Street was another one of his beats, and the handball courts. Sleepers are in copious supply, often in grotesque postures. As for workers on the job, Levinstein doesn't show them except at the end of his life when he goes to Haiti and India and brings back pictures of backbreaking labor.

In an obvious sense, his brief transit in the Third World had been well prepared by his experience as a native in the Big Apple. His career coincides with a great wave of immigration to the city over the last thirty years that increased its population of Hispanics, Asiatics, and Eastern Europeans. Just as it was individuals rather than the corporate mass that attracted him, so it was the ethnics, and blacks, rather than the Anglos, upon whom he focused. Certainly the vibrancy of these "others" offered greater visual dividends to him, as it did to many New York photographers. More importantly, the immigrants lived in a complex state in which they were both assimilated to and excluded by the host culture, as were all minorities in the polyglot atmosphere. By virtue of being an itinerant photographer Levinstein was an outsider to whatever group he came upon; but because he was also a first-generation Jewish American (who had been raised in a West Virginia town), he could identify with the immigrant experience in a particularly emphatic way. The city exists as a scenario in which no one specifically belongs, but all can live. Their acceptance of this condition typified people as New Yorkers before it became common elsewhere. For someone who ambles for visual material through the streets, life appears extremely heterogeneous, filled with enclaves that encroach upon each other but do not mix. In short, the spectacle offered is parochial, the very opposite of the cosmopolitanism signified by modernity.

The time had long passed in cultural history when New York could be understood and celebrated as the headquarters of modernism, or at least, the progressive. The myth of the city as a capital of our century – a dynamo of commerce, industry, and finance – had been collectively evoked by Alfred Steiglitz, Edward Steichen, Paul Strand, Charles Sheeler, and Margaret Bourke-White. But this myth did not survive the Depression. A hopeful future symbolized by the skyscrapers was replaced by an often elegiac look at the city's small businesses and their roots in a nineteenth-century mercantilism. It's enough to think of the photography of Walker Evans and Berenice Abbott, American realists whose work reflects a European sense of the past.

But the specifically Jewish contribution to the photographic picturing of New York remains the most archetypal because it was the most sympathetic to the city's role as crossroads or induction center, and maybe proving ground, for newcomers, where the stresses of continuing immigrant experience made themselves felt. The Jewish photographers turned New York into a public arena, where culture shock and accommodation, in successive waves, were the order of the day. It was as if, before they could affect a larger audience, these picturemakers had to explain the city and all its people to brethren in terms familiar to their own consciousness. This theme of a metropolis that remakes its citizens, even as they retain their diversity and keep their edginess, has won through in the history of photography. The worldwide import of New York is bound up with such a drama that was first visualized in epic form by Lewis Hine, who took it upon himself to document the arrival of untold, scared thousands as they got off the boat at Ellis Island.

More is put in question here, of course, than a phenomenon of civics. If there is such a thing as being at home with displacement, the Jews were experts in it. Small-town America was ostensibly placid, wholesome, Republican, and Wasp. Manhattan, being the opposite, was therefore regarded as suspect in its nationality. Perhaps because they themselves often came from dispersed and stateless backgrounds, or underneath felt only provisionally settled, Jewish photographers were sensitive to this amazing, high-density no-man's-land called New York. In the '40s, Helen Levitt conceived the streets as compressed and makeshift havens for small communities. And Weegee saw those same thoroughfares as theatres of mob rub-outs and carnivals of tabloid misfortune. In the '50s, Robert Frank viewed New York as a staging area for footloose newcomers, anonymous drab work, and questionable subcultures. For his part, William Klein depicted the place as an oppressive landscape of jittery but quite deadening signs – corporate media at their most inhuman. Viewing all their images, one reckons with the city's toll upon the life of its people, and a kind of pride the photographers take in their unsparing observance. Even more, the critique they offer of this urban environment does not exclude the affection they feel for it – as a site of their own longing for identity.

Such was the practice from which Leon Levinstein emerged and then added his distinctive note. He had become acquainted with the Photo League, an association of streetshooters with proletarian sympathies, who worked the neighborhoods. Later, he studied with one of the photographers there, Sid Grossman, who held private workshops. This was the late '40s. From all accounts an effective pedagogue, given to formalist talk, Grossman was something of a lyrical expressionist in his own imagery. Much of Grossman's grunge and froth was successfully extended in Levinstein's later work – but the student wanted something more solid. With Grossman, a visceral empathy with the collective emotion of beach or festival was often suffused in atmospherics. By the evidence of his own work, Levinstein charges this interest in phenomena – caused by movement of the camera, approximate focus, and low light – with a kind of emotional kineticism. It was not as if he supposed that one could photograph a feeling. But his own apprehension as a photographer could be made to dramatize the pictorial mode of address as something importunate, searching, perhaps even dangerous.

It's significant that while he obviously possessed an immediate photographic culture, among those who affected him Levinstein cited two *painters* in particular: Reginald Marsh and Edvard Munch. The first reference tells us something about a caricatural element that runs through the photographer's work, manifested in the exaggeration of human forms. The second speaks to us of his interest in faces as icons or masks that concentrate and therefore give some extremity to an emotional tone. We don't as yet know enough about Levinstein to consider this caricatural/symbolic input as a programmatic feature of his outlook. But it is idiomatic enough. Certainly he picked up on city types whom he formulated as characters, and then often showed them as possessed by a mood. It can be as extreme as in Weegee, a true photographic caricaturist, but without the hysteria that so often afflicts Weegee's victims. Whatever seems to animate Levinstein's people is the chance product of his unnoticed encounter with them, at a fortuitous or irrelevant moment, and not – as far as we can guess – a result of their circumstances. It is mysterious or it can suddenly brighten; it fluctuates in arbitrary currents that convey the most nervous sense of life on the streets.

With a kind of bogus involvement that is nevertheless extremely tense, the photographer introduces us to scenes that lack any anecdotal value. The fact that he had closed with strangers does not in any sense soften our or their defenses. If anything, such short pictorial range increases a barrier effect. Something is wrong about the visual proximity; it's too abrupt and unexplained. It would seem that the main interest is physiognomic, but a conventional portrait effect is the last thing suggested by these outdoor pictures that do not tell us much about the street, either. Levinstein probes so as to electrify the picture, not to investigate personality. Strangely enough, one seems to learn more about people through their hands or gestures than their faces. A viewer eventually figures that abstraction is both a necessary aesthetic structure to this work, and an obstacle to empathy with its subjects.

He spoke in his interview of his desire to be clear, and yet there are moments when the clear visual effect produces an image that is psychologically hard to read. A characteristic pattern of ordering allows him to avoid the merely random impressions endemic to the street mode. At the same time, it countermanded a sentimental tendency, obscuring most if not all those moments when he might have been disarmed in the presence of human casualties. Meanwhile, his latent sense of abstraction also worked to neutralize any satiric facility, occasionally just under the surface of his pictures. On this level, Levinstein is to be distinguished from Lisette Model and her student Diane Arbus. They achieved some of their most gripping pictures unhindered by a regard for the dignity of their subjects, the younger artist here going further at the expense of those she photographed than the older. Levinstein lacked both the European, bohemian culture of the one colleague and the privileged economic background of the other. With a kind of brilliant slumming, they pictured the social underside of what for him was the pervasive reality of the city. They penetrated downward; he mingled horizontally. But his innate structuralism might just the same have reflected a dream of upward mobility . . . the fulfilment of an artistic mission that sailed high above the regional in a modernist synthesis of forms.

From our vantage, such a goal looks as if it originated in the Constructivist aesthetic of the '20s. It had struck Edward Steichen as humanist enough to be included in *The Family of Man* at the Museum of Modern Art in 1955. Were it to have been noticed in group shows of the '60s, Levinstein's work could have been judged understandably – and mistakenly – as old left. And by the '70s, he swam very much against the tide of disenchantment in the prolix descriptions and deliberately overstated randomness of Garry Winogrand and Lee Friedlander. Their triumphant view of the city (and the small town, for that matter) as an accretion of meaningless pop culture had passed him by. Juxtaposed with them, he affirmed a more singular vision that was time-warped in its internal conflicts.

Levinstein's art enlarged upon nominally small incident. His problem was to make the whole of the frame count as an energized field, even as he was focused on only one passage – the fullness of someone's belly, gnarled fingers, an open mouth, a wild gaze. Nothing would have rivaled such details in articulateness, but they themselves did not comprise a picture. His feeling for larger zones and masses, particularly if they kept the viewer off balance, came to the rescue. Occasionally, the solution of the problem was technical, and resulted in effective icons. But there occur other moments, too, when everything fuses in such an incisive way that viewers feel that they are locked into the scene – are at one with its passion. Such were the times when the city came into its own and a stubborn career was vindicated.

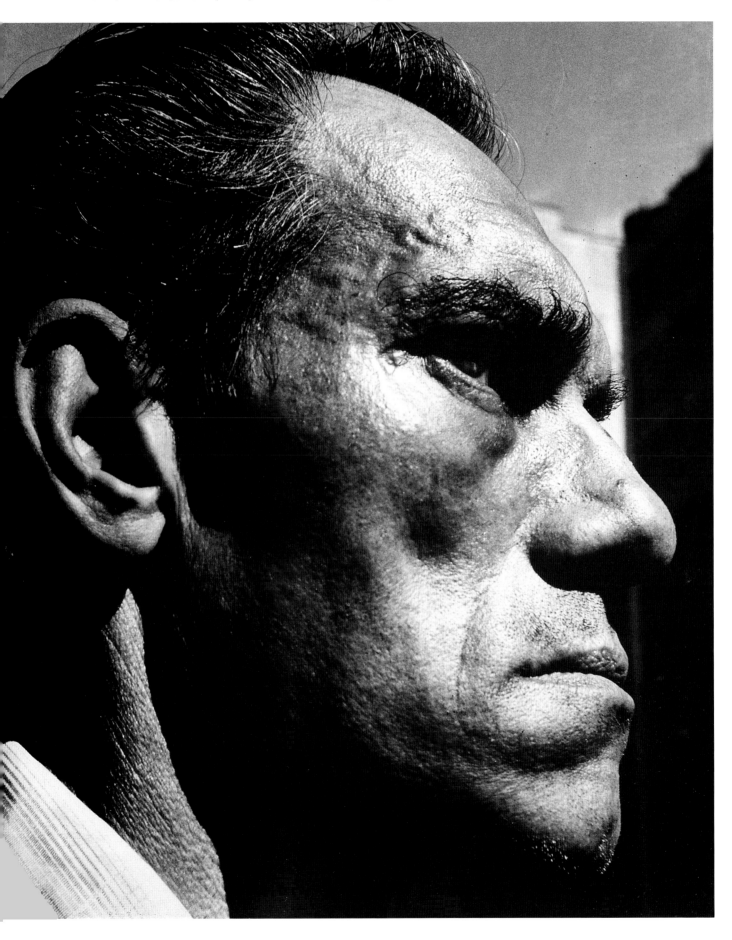

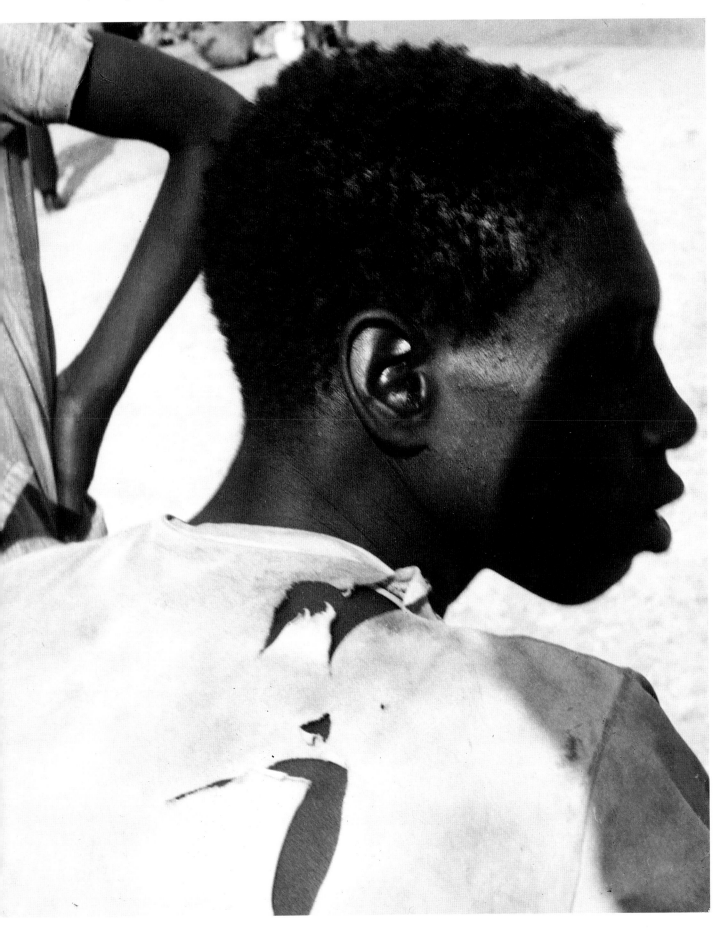

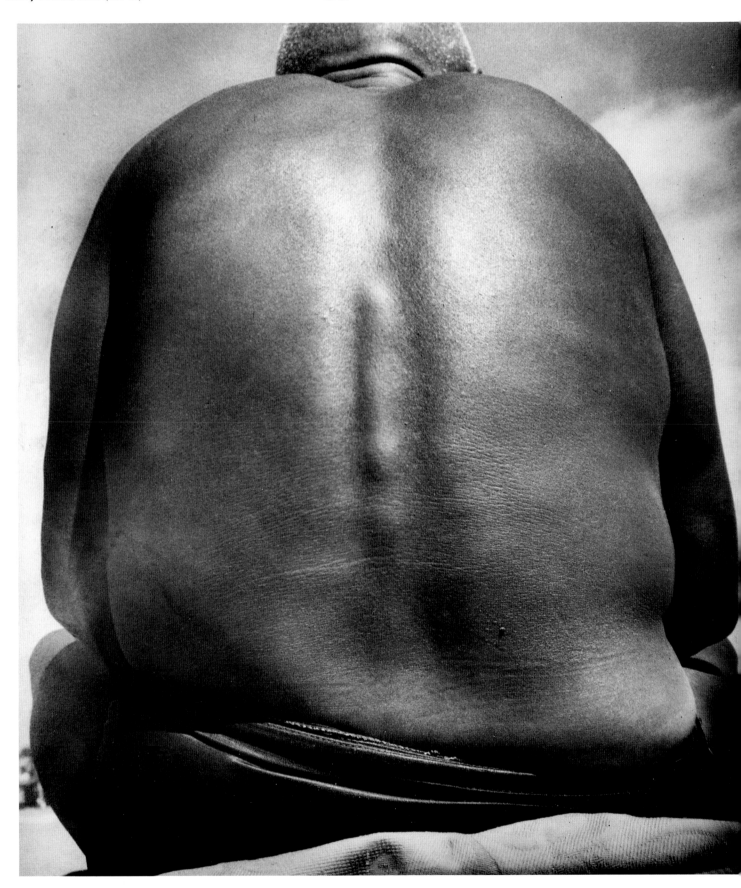

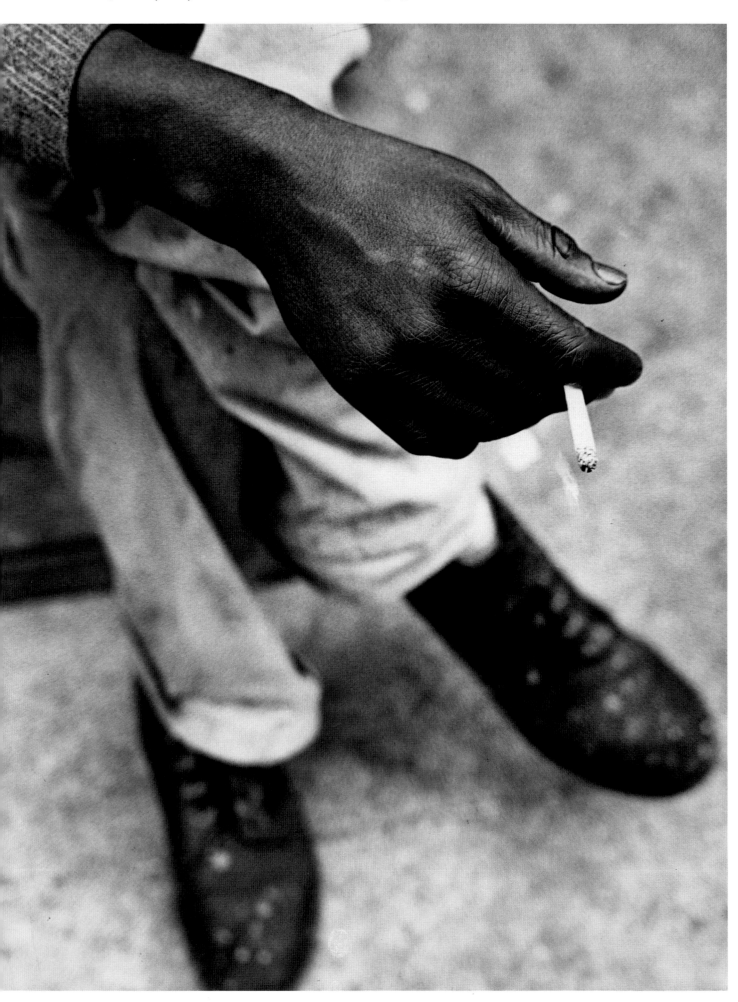

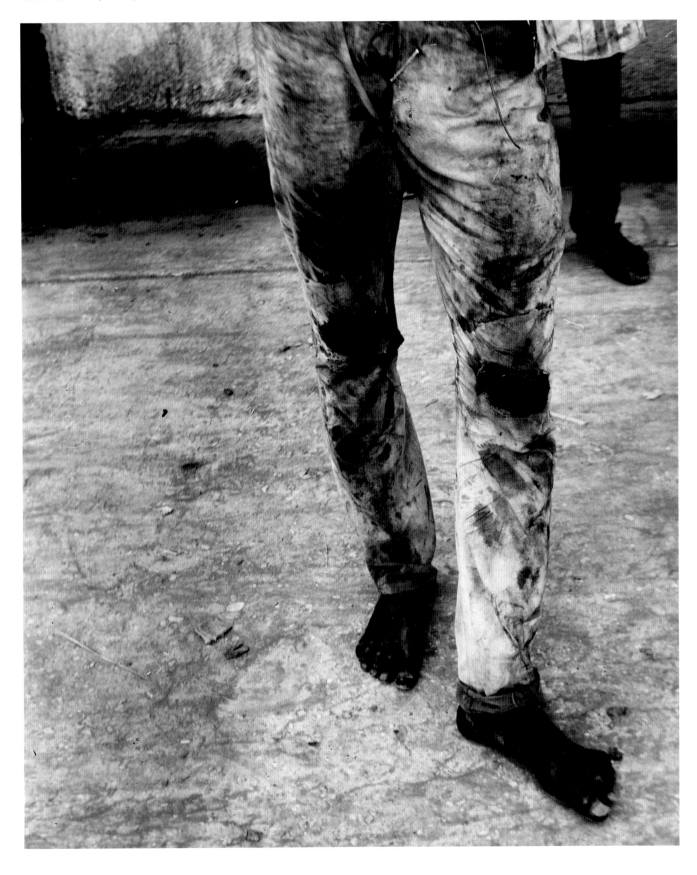

CATALOGUE

Titles in italics are taken from Levinstein's own inscriptions; titles in roman are those that have been assigned by the owner of the work; the phrases in parentheses are not titles but simply descriptions of the contents of the image. All works are on gelatin silver paper. Measurements refer to image size; height precedes width. Works from the collection of Stuart E. Karu are courtesy of the Howard Greenberg Gallery, New York.

1
Untitled (horse)
c. 1950
34.8 × 27.8 cm
National Gallery of Canada (36661)

2
Untitled (woman in the street gazing upward)
1950s
27.4 × 34.7 cm
Stuart E. Karu

3
Untitled (older woman in profile with a veil)
1950s
28.1 × 35.4 cm
Stuart E. Karu

4
Untitled (woman with a veil and pearls)
1950s?
35.4 × 28.2 cm
Sander Gallery, New York

5
Untitled (man counting his change)
between 1950 and 1965
35.4 × 28.2 cm
Sander Gallery, New York

6
Untitled (bearded man reading a Yiddish newspaper, Lower East Side)
1951
34.7 × 26.5 cm
Stuart E. Karu

7
Rockefeller Center (man's head, with a hat, in profile against a skyscraper)
1952
26.7 × 32.4 cm
Martin Bondell and Juliette Galant, New York

8
Coney Island (swirling skirt and a couple on the beach)
1952
26.6 × 34.4 cm
National Gallery of Canada, gift of the American Friends of Canada Committee, Inc., through the generosity of Stuart E. Karu

9
Harlem (blind woman with a tin cup)
c. 1952
33.5 × 28.2 cm
National Gallery of Canada, gift of the American Friends of Canada Committee, Inc., through the generosity of Stuart E. Karu

10
Lower East Side, New York City
(close-up of two men)
c. 1952 (printed c. 1980)
34.6 × 41.8 cm
National Gallery of Canada (36653)

11
Prospect Park (Orthodox Jewish man lying under a tree)
1954
27.2 × 34.9 cm
Dreyfus Corporation, New York

12
Untitled (man and a woman with a fur coat, East 57th Street)
1954
41.9 × 38.9 cm
Stuart E. Karu

13
Coney Island (large man's back)
1955
30.1 × 26.5 cm
National Gallery of Canada (35079)

14
Coney Island (head and shoulders of a couple lying together)
1955
28.0 × 35.6 cm
National Gallery of Canada, gift of the American Friends of Canada Committee, Inc., through the generosity of Stuart E. Karu

15
Coney Island (man in bathing trunks asleep on the beach)
c. 1955 (printed c. 1980)
32.0 × 46.3 cm
Stuart E. Karu

16
Coney Island (woman in a flowered shirt and a man reclining on the beach)
c. 1955
27.4 × 35.2 cm
National Gallery of Canada (35061)
Shown only in Ottawa

17
Coney Island (back view of a man seated under the boardwalk holding a young girl)
c. 1955
35.2 × 27.9 cm
Stuart E. Karu

18
Coney Island (father and daughter lying on the beach)
c. 1955
32.0 × 42.2 cm
Stuart E. Karu

19
Coney Island (standing man and seated woman at the beach)
c. 1955
41.1 × 37.8 cm
National Gallery of Canada (36659)

20
Lower East Side, New York (couple in profile in a car)
c. 1955
27.7 × 35.5 cm
National Gallery of Canada, gift of the American Friends of Canada Committee, Inc., through the generosity of Stuart E. Karu

21
Untitled (stout man with suspenders under the El, New York)
c. 1955
33.0 × 27.8 cm
Stuart E. Karu

22
Untitled (close-up of hand with cigarette, Lower East Side)
c. 1955
35.3 × 27.8 cm
John Erdman and Gary Schneider, New York

23
Untitled (head and shoulders profile of a man in a work shirt)
c. 1955
34.9 × 27.8 cm
National Gallery of Canada (36656)

24
Untitled (couple lying on a blanket)
c. 1955
26.7 × 34.0 cm
Hallmark Cards, Inc., Kansas City, Missouri

25
Prospect Park (Orthodox Jewish family reclining under the trees)
c. 1955 (printed c. 1980)
28.1 × 48.9 cm
Stuart E. Karu

26
Untitled (man holding a hat, Mexico)
between 1955 and 1963
34.5 × 27.7 cm
Stuart E. Karu

27
Untitled (blind beggar holding a hat, Mexico)
between 1955 and 1963
34.6 × 36.8 cm
Stuart E. Karu

28
Untitled (entwined hands of a man and woman)
between 1955 and 1965
27.7 × 25.3 cm
Stuart E. Karu

29
Rockefeller Center (profile of two older women with hats)
1956
41.5 × 34.5 cm
National Gallery of Canada, gift of the American Friends of Canada Committee, Inc., through the generosity of Stuart E. Karu

30
Harlem (close-up of a man's head with cloth cap)
c. 1956
40.0 × 40.5 cm
National Gallery of Canada (36654)

31
Untitled (man in front of a shop window with reflections)
c. 1957
27.1 × 33.6 cm
Stuart E. Karu

32
Prospect Park (back view of a couple with cigarettes)
1958
35.1 × 27.0 cm
Art Institute of Chicago
1990.354

33
Untitled (tattooed man, Coney Island)
1958
49.4 × 39.5 cm
National Gallery of Canada, gift of the American Friends of Canada Committee, Inc., through the generosity of Stuart E. Karu

34
Coney Island (back view of a man with suspenders combing his hair)
c. 1958
35.4 × 28.0 cm
Stuart E. Karu

35
Coney Island (back view of two men with shaved heads)
1959 (printed c. 1980)
39.5 × 48.6 cm
Stuart E. Karu

36
Coney Island (two young men with tattoos talking to women)
c. 1959
27.9 × 34.4 cm
National Gallery of Canada, gift of the American Friends of Canada Committee, Inc., through the generosity of Stuart E. Karu

37
Fifth Avenue (back view of a man with a bowler hat)
c. 1959
26.8 × 33.9 cm
Stuart E. Karu

38
Untitled (man standing on edge of sidewalk, head cropped)
1960 (printed 1977?)
35.0 × 34.7 cm
Metropolitan Museum of Art, New York (1994.3)

39
Untitled (young couple embracing)
c. 1960
31.8 × 27.8 cm
Dreyfus Corporation, New York

40
Untitled (man with a plaid cloth cap)
c. 1960
26.4 × 37.5 cm
Dreyfus Corporation, New York

41
Untitled (reclining man with arms crossed over his head, Coney Island)
1960s
36.0 × 40.1 cm
National Gallery of Canada, gift of the American Friends of Canada Committee, Inc., through the generosity of Stuart E. Karu

42
Untitled (two large women in print dresses)
1960s
34.9 × 27.5 cm
Stuart E. Karu

43
Untitled (man with sunglasses, with head tilted back)
between 1960 and 1975
33.3 × 27.9 cm
National Gallery of Canada, gift of the American Friends of Canada Committee, Inc., through the generosity of Stuart E. Karu

44
New York (children playing in the water)
1962
34.4 × 27.0 cm
National Gallery of Canada, gift of the American Friends of Canada Committee, Inc., through the generosity of Stuart E. Karu

45
Lower East Side (man holding a doll)
1964
35.2 × 27.9 cm
Stuart E. Karu

46
Untitled (Speakers' Corner, Hyde Park, London)
1964?
26.2 × 32.7 cm
Stuart E. Karu

47
Untitled (clown napping in his dressing room)
c. 1964
43.2 × 32.0 cm
Stuart E. Karu

48
Coney Island (back view of a man with his arm on another man's shoulder)
c. 1965
36.8 × 34.9 cm
National Gallery of Canada, gift of the American Friends of Canada Committee, Inc., through the generosity of Stuart E. Karu

49
Untitled (woman in profile holding a baby)
1965
41.3 × 31.7 cm
Sander Gallery, New York

50
Untitled (seated man holding a reclining woman at the beach)
1965
31.9 × 36.5 cm
National Gallery of Canada (36655)

51
New Year's Eve, Times Square (man with upraised arms in a crowd)
c. 1965
33.1 × 48.0 cm
National Gallery of Canada, gift of the American Friends of Canada Committee, Inc., through the generosity of Stuart E. Karu

52
Lower East Side (group of four girls)
c. 1965
32.1 × 27.1 cm
National Gallery of Canada, gift of the
American Friends of Canada Committee,
Inc., through the generosity of Stuart E. Karu

53
Untitled (young woman holding a cigar,
leaning against the corner of a building)
c. 1965
31.6 × 26.2 cm
Dreyfus Corporation, New York

54
Untitled (man leaning on a railing)
c. 1965
28.8 × 26.9 cm
National Gallery of Canada, gift of the
American Friends of Canada Committee,
Inc., through the generosity of Stuart E. Karu

55
Lower East Side, Bowery (man with a
suitcase)
c. 1965
35.5 × 28.2 cm
National Gallery of Canada, gift of the
American Friends of Canada Committee,
Inc., through the generosity of Stuart E. Karu

56
Untitled (young man holding his head)
between 1965 and 1975
35.4 × 28.2 cm
National Gallery of Canada, gift of the
American Friends of Canada Committee,
Inc., through the generosity of Stuart E. Karu

57
Untitled (man in the street looking at
a woman wearing hot pants)
between 1965 and 1975
28.1 × 35.4 cm
Stuart E. Karu

58
East Village (seated woman with her
hands in her lap)
1966
27.7 × 27.3 cm
Stuart E. Karu

59
Fifth Avenue, New York (close-up profile
of a man's face)
c. 1969
41.2 × 34.4 cm
National Gallery of Canada (35060)

60
Houston Street, New York ("Handball
Players")
1970 (printed c. 1980)
45.6 × 35.6 cm
National Gallery of Canada (36664)

61
Untitled (street scene with head of a man
against the sky)
c. 1970
28.1 × 35.4 cm
National Gallery of Canada, gift of the
American Friends of Canada Committee,
Inc., through the generosity of Stuart E. Karu

62
Coney Island (back view of a woman in
a floral jacket and a man in striped pants
holding hands)
c. 1970
27.5 × 25.5 cm
Stuart E. Karu

63
Coney Island (legs of a couple standing
on the beach)
c. 1970
34.4 × 26.8 cm
Stuart E. Karu

64
Untitled (back view of a woman in hot
pants and a man in a checkered suit)
c. 1970
26.8 × 34.5 cm
Stuart E. Karu

65
Untitled (man unloading carcasses, Haiti)
1970s
32.5 × 26.1 cm
Stuart E. Karu

66
Untitled (profile of a young man's head, Haiti)
1970s
31.7 × 26.1 cm
National Gallery of Canada, gift of the American Friends of Canada Committee, Inc., through the generosity of Stuart E. Karu

67
Untitled (woman washing, Haiti)
1970s
33.4 × 23.7 cm
National Gallery of Canada, gift of the American Friends of Canada Committee, Inc., through the generosity of Stuart E. Karu

68
Untitled (man's legs, Haiti)
1970s
33.3 × 26.9 cm
National Gallery of Canada, gift of the American Friends of Canada Committee, Inc., through the generosity of Stuart E. Karu

69
Untitled (man with a sack draped over his head, Haiti)
1970s
35.4 × 28.0 cm
Stuart E. Karu

70
Untitled (woman carrying a chair, Haiti)
1970s
24.2 × 35.3 cm
Stuart E. Karu

71
Haiti (close-up of an elderly man and his shadow)
1970s
35.2 × 27.7 cm
Stuart E. Karu

72
Untitled (close-up of a man's hands crossed behind his back)
1970s
35.4 × 28.1 cm
Stuart E. Karu

73
Untitled (man and a woman in front of a stage show poster)
1970s
34.1 × 26.6 cm
Stuart E. Karu

74
Untitled (man shielding his face with his arm)
1970s
35.0 × 27.5 cm
Sander Gallery, New York

75
Broadway and 42nd Street (standing thin man and his shadow)
1970s
41.8 × 31.2 cm
National Gallery of Canada, gift of the American Friends of Canada Committee, Inc., through the generosity of Stuart E. Karu

76
Untitled (three men standing at a bar)
1970s?
35.3 × 43.1 cm
Stuart E. Karu

77
Untitled (men gesturing with their hands)
between 1970 and 1985
35.0 × 25.8 cm
Sander Gallery, New York

78
Central Park, New York (close-up of a young woman embraced by a man)
1974
32.9 × 26.5 cm
National Gallery of Canada (36662)

79
Eighth Avenue and 41st Street, Times Square (woman standing at subway entrance)
1975
35.1 × 26.2 cm
National Gallery of Canada (36657)

80
Untitled (young man wearing a G-string at a Mardi Gras)
1975
41.9 × 31.4 cm
National Gallery of Canada, gift of the American Friends of Canada Committee, Inc., through the generosity of Stuart E. Karu

81
Fifth Avenue (transvestite wearing a blond wig)
c. 1975
35.5 × 28.1 cm
Dr. Barry Ramer, Santa Rosa, California

82
Untitled (man standing outside an adult bookstore, Los Angeles)
c. 1975
34.6 × 26.7 cm
National Gallery of Canada, gift of the American Friends of Canada Committee, Inc., through the generosity of Stuart E. Karu

83
Times Square (woman in hot pants and white stockings talking to a man)
1979
42.0 × 31.4 cm
Stuart E. Karu

84
Untitled (close-up of three youths)
c. 1979 (printed c. 1980)
39.3 × 48.8 cm
Stuart E. Karu

85
Untitled (seated man, India)
c. 1980
33.1 × 25.1 cm
Stuart E. Karu

86
Untitled (girl leading a man, India)
c. 1980
27.6 × 35.2 cm
Brick Store Museum, Kennebunk, Maine

87
42nd Street, Times Square (man and a woman at entrance to a peep show)
c. 1980
41.8 × 34.6 cm
Stuart E. Karu

88
42nd Street and Eighth Avenue (two men at an outdoor food counter)
1984
49.2 × 39.4 cm
Stuart E. Karu

EXHIBITIONS

1952
Then and Now
Museum of Modern Art, New York

1953
Always the Young Strangers
Museum of Modern Art, New York

**The Exhibition of Contemporary
Photography – Japan and America**
National Museum of Modern Art, Tokyo

1955
The Family of Man
Museum of Modern Art, New York

**Seven Photographers Look at
New York**
A Photographer's Gallery, New York

14 Photographers
Limelight Gallery, New York

1956
Levinstein's New York
Limelight Gallery, New York

1957
**Seventy Photographers Look at
New York**
Museum of Modern Art, New York

1958
**Photographs from the Museum
Collection**
Museum of Modern Art, New York

1959
Group Show
Limelight Gallery, New York

1960
Photographs for Collectors
Museum of Modern Art, New York

A Bid for Space – Part II
Museum of Modern Art, New York

1964
The Photographer's Eye
Museum of Modern Art, New York

1965
**About New York, Night and Day,
1915–1965**
Gallery of Modern Art, New York

1967
The Camera as Witness
Expo 67, Montreal

1969
Harlem on My Mind
Metropolitan Museum of Art, New York

1973
The Jew in New York
Midtown Y Gallery, New York

1977
**Helen Gee and the Limelight:
A Pioneering Photography Gallery
of the Fifties**
Carlton Gallery, New York

1978
**New Standpoints: Photography
1940–1955**
Museum of Modern Art, New York

Group Show
Floating Foundation of Photography,
New York

1980

**Photography of the Fifties:
An American Perspective**

Center for Creative Photography, Tucson
International Center of Photography,
New York

1982

Leon Levinstein

Light Gallery, New York

1985

**American Images: Photography
1945–1980**

Barbican Art Gallery, London

**The New York School: Photographs,
1935–1963, Part III**

Corcoran Gallery of Art, Washington, D.C.

1990

Leon Levinstein

Photofind Gallery, New York

1991

**Photography from the 1940s and
1950s: Selections from the
Collection**

Metropolitan Museum of Art, New York

**Sid Grossman/Leon Levinstein: New
York Street Photographers**

San Francisco Museum of Modern Art

**Mean Streets: American
Photographs from the Collection,
1940s–1980s**

Museum of Modern Art, New York

1992

**Black through Time: Photographs of
Black Urban Life 1937–1973, by
Louis Faurer, Leon Levinstein, Helen
Levitt**

Bayly Art Museum, University of Virginia,
Charlottesville

**Troubled Times . . . : An Exhibition
of Vintage Photographs by Louis
Faurer, Leon Levinstein, Lisette
Model**

Sander Gallery, New York

1994

**The Street Walkers: Leon Levinstein
and Frank Paulin**

Howard Greenberg Gallery, New York

PERMANENT COLLECTIONS

Art Institute of Chicago
Australian National Gallery, Canberra
Center for Creative Photography, Tucson
Consolidated Freightways, Palo Alto
Dreyfus Corporation, New York
Hallmark Cards, Kansas City
Los Angeles County Museum of Art
Metropolitan Museum of Art, New York
Museum of Fine Arts, Houston
Museum Folkwang, Essen, Germany
Museum of Modern Art, New York
National Gallery of Canada, Ottawa
New Orleans Museum of Art
San Francisco Museum of Modern Art

BIBLIOGRAPHY

B O O K S   A N D   A R T I C L E S

Benton-Harris, John. "Leon Levinstein, 1913–1988." *Creative Camera*, July 1989, pp. 18–19.

Charlottesville, Bayly Art Museum, University of Virginia. *Black through Time: Photographs of Black Urban Life 1937–1973*. Text by Stephen Margulies. 1992.

"Coney Island." Photographs selected by Grace M. Mayer. *Camera*, March 1971, pp. 6–45.

Deschin, Jacob. "'Family of Man': Museum of Modern Art Prepares Global Collection for January Opening." *New York Times*, 12 December 1954.

Deschin, Jacob. "Focusing on People." *New York Times*, 8 January 1956, section 2, p. 21.

"Dreams Deferred." *New Yorker*, 23 November 1992, p. 31.

The Family of Woman. New York: Ridge Press / Grosset & Dunlap, 1979.

Fell, John Louis. Review of the exhibition "Then and Now" at the Museum of Modern Art, New York. *Photo Arts*, December 1952, pp. 426–33.

Fonvielle, Lloyd. "The City's Lively Beat: A Spirited New York Exhibit Rediscovers Street Photography 1940–1955." *Aperture*, no. 81, 1978, pp. 60–73.

Gee, Helen. *Photography of the Fifties: An American Perspective*. Tucson: Center for Creative Photography, University of Arizona, 1980.

Gee, Helen. "Where the Life Is." *Camera Arts*, March/April 1982, pp. 50–63.

Hagen, Charles. "A City Defines a Style and Perhaps Vice Versa." *New York Times*, 20 November 1992, section C, p. 29.

H.K. "Review of an Exhibit: 500 Photographs from the Collection of the Museum of Modern Art." *Modern Photography*, March 1959, pp. 60–61, 102, 118.

"Leon Levinstein." *U.S. Camera 1956*, pp. 255, 262–67.

Lifson, Ben. "The 50s: Happy Daze." *Village Voice*, 2 July 1980, p. 62.

Livingston, Jane. *The New York School: Photographs 1936–1963*. New York: Stewart, Tabori and Chang, 1992.

Montreal, Expo 67. *International Exhibition of Photography: The Camera as Witness*. 1967.

New York, Carlton Gallery. *Helen Gee and the Limelight: A Pioneering Photography Gallery of the Fifties*. 1977.

New York, Gallery of Modern Art. *About New York, Night and Day, 1915–1965*. 1965.

New York, Midtown Y Gallery. *The Jew in New York*. 1973.

New York, Photofind Gallery. *Leon Levinstein*. Text by Helen Gee. 1990.

Nixon, Bruce. "Street Scenes: Sid Grossman and Leon Levinstein at SFMOMA." *Artweek*, 21 February 1991, p. 13.

Photography of the World. 2 volumes. Tokyo: Heibonsha Publishers, 1958.

Stathatos, John. "Curating 'American Images': An Interview with Peter Turner." *Creative Camera*, May 1985, pp. 26–31.

Steichen, Edward. *The Family of Man*. New York: Simon and Schuster / Maco Magazine Corporation, 1955.

Szarkowski, John. *The Photographer's Eye*. New York: Museum of Modern Art, 1966.

Tokyo, National Museum of Modern Art. *The Exhibition of Contemporary Photography – Japan and America*. Introduction by Edward Steichen. 1953.

Turner, Peter, ed. *American Images: Photography 1945–1980*. New York: Viking, 1985.

Turner, Peter. *History of Photography*. Greenwich, Conn.: Brompton, 1987.

Wright, George B. "Levinstein at Limelight: 'Powerful Group of Photos,'" *Village Voice*, 11 January 1956, p. 9.

PHOTOGRAPHY ANNUALS

U.S. Camera Annual 1951, p. 337.

U.S. Camera Annual 1952, pp. 49, 61.

Photography Annual 1952 (by the editors of *Popular Photography*), pp. 61, 117.

Photography Annual 1953 (by the editors of *Popular Photography*), p. 111.

Photography Annual 1955 (by the editors of *Popular Photography*) , pp. 180, 208–09, 225.

Photography Annual 1956 (by the editors of *Popular Photography*), pp. 115, 130–31.

Photography Annual 1957 (by the editors of *Popular Photography*), p. 65.

U.S. Camera 1957, pp. 52–53.

U.S. Camera International Pictures 1964, p. 103.